Re: Action

STUDIO HANI RASHID
University of Applied Arts Vienna

edition:ˈʌngewʌndtə
Universität für angewandte Kunst Wien
University of Applied Arts Vienna

Edition Angewandte
Book Series of the University of Applied Arts Vienna
Edited by Gerald Bast, Rector

Re:Action

Urban Resilience, Sustainable Growth,
and the Vitality of Cities and Ecosystems
in the Post-Information Age

Birkhäuser
Basel

Hani Rashid (Ed.)

TABLE OF CONTENTS

INTRO

Hani Rashid

Activating Agency

PROJECTS

01 Paradigm_Park
02 Oceanic_Urbanism
03 Bio_Materials
04 Intelligent_Architecture

PANEL TALK

Anab Jain, Greg Lynn, Timothy Morton, Claudia Pasquero, Hani Rashid

Corrective Methodologies and Architectural Futures

ESSAY

Lenia Mascha

Ec(o)centric Form

ESSAY

Sophie Luger

Re: Resilience

PROJECTS

05 Smart_Systems
06 Energy_Networks
07 Transactive_Landscapes
08 Urban Agro_Culture

APPENDIX

Biographies
Students
Imprint

Studio Hani Rashid

8

12
44
76
110

148

172

174

176
202
230
264

286
290
292

Silvia Nanu, Adriana Böck, Harry Hinton-Hard, Hani Rashid

Thesis Presentation by Shilun Yang, 2020

6 Studio Hani Rashid

Hani Rashid, Greg Lynn, Kazuyo Sejima

Thesis Presentation by Luca Melchiori, 2019

Activating Agency

Hani Rashid

The past five years witnessed some quite dramatic and unprecedented events worldwide. Not the least is the global pandemic, the war in Ukraine, Trump's America, and the precarious teetering from right to left in European politics. Today I am writing this during an unprecedented heat wave, which much of the planet is attempting to deal with. Global warming, rising sea levels, water scarcity, virus mutations, and other related and unrelated global problems today impact every–one and everything and in particular our cities. Despite the unfathomable scale and weightiness of the ongoing troubling situations with the planet's health, we must ask some crucial and straightforward questions, particularly from within our discipline as architects. What can archi-tecture bring to the table regarding the current and future situation when considering dramatic climate change and the implications of globalization? Can this discipline that questionably has fallen victim to stylistic Instagram-inspired one-liners rise again to have some semblance of an authentic voice of authority that is trusted and, more importantly, heard?

This discipline's long and profound history is no stranger to dramatic change, obsolescence, and fashion. After World War II, visionary and inspired architects worked alongside brilliant structural engineers to devise new and radical ways of thinking about architecture and game-changing strategies and approaches. From long-span structures to eliminating unnecessary motifs and super–fluous ornamentation and, above all else, streamlining the cumbersome and convoluted building process of the time. So, with unprecedented efficiency and primarily driven by economic necessity, high modernism was born. Since those halcyon days, we have seen the profession slip into a fog-like persona and existence. Postmodernism, deconstructivism, and the branded "star architects" of the late '90s and early '00s have all come and gone quite rapidly, leaving in their wake some uncertainty but, more importantly, a new openness and freedom for a whole new generation of young architects to find their footing again and produce projects that might be untethered to marketing strategies and popularity.

Architecture is a massively influential art form at its core. And increasingly, the profession's actual impact on the public realm is not from up high in the academies and schools but rather from the foot soldiers, the small firms, and individual architects who are creating new types of multidisciplinary "practices" that set out to engage com-munities and the public at large with radical and discursive ideas and possibilities for the future. These self-imposed "silo practices," set in places and cities around the globe, exert a bottom-up influence on the discipline crucial to architecture's future and purpose. This new modality of practicing architecture is most successful when situated precisely at the nexus of art and science. Despite some of the propaganda that technologists hold all the cards, especially when tackling the significant issues of our time, it is ultimately that architectural innovations will have the most tangible and profound impact on societies and, therefore, on the future of our cities and lives.

In this light, this book has been put together as a compilation of some intriguing, profound, sublime, problematic, and perplexing works executed by my master's degree students with the assistance of my outstanding teaching staff at the Angewandte in Vienna. The works and texts on these pages were carried out in the past five years. They are not merely "student works" or academic ivory tower exercises. Instead, they are deeply researched and superbly executed ideas, drawings, models, proposals, masterplans, and schemes that are all viable and considered alternative solutions to genuine and compelling problems in our collective push to the future. The projects not only tackle architectural methodologies and question standards, they also pave the way to defining new forms of practice and, by extension, a redefinition of the architect's role going forward.

In reality, this book offers few, if any, immediate answers. Instead, the projects highlighted here have been produced in the spirit of experimentation and discovery. Moreover, even as these projects shed stark and, at times, disturbing light on some very severe and pressing issues, they also are stunning. These works' brilliance and aesthetic beauty should not be misconstrued as being without depth and logic. Instead, the more stunning the visuals, the more profound the arguments being made. Then again, some of the works are purposely less aesthetically compelling and perhaps even a little disturbing, but they also should be appreciated for their critical polemics and depth of reasoning.

It does not matter on which side these works sit in the art versus engineering spectrum. The key is that they all confront both the ills and charms of technological progress and human need. Furthermore, through some profound insights and probing, they collectively point the way to some intriguing possibilities for the evolution of the discipline, a shapeshift of sorts toward being an active agent of change instead of a passive observer of the present. Undoubtedly architecture, as a discipline, will regain its powerful cultural station, especially as we consider that architecture has much less to do with building buildings and a great deal more to do with forging innovative and groundbreaking options for the future of our cities and, above all, for the much-needed repairs to our fragile and stoic mothership, Earth.

Hani Rashid
New York City _ Urbino, Italy
2022

Crit Session with Hani Rashid

Seri
Fu

Studio Hani Rashid

ous
in

In reference to the *Serious-Fun* oil on cardboard painting from Wassily Kandinsky from 1930 and Laurie Anderson's concert at the Serious Fun Festival at Lincoln Center in 1988. (Image © Roswitha Janowski-Fritsch)

01

Paradigm_Park

Paradigm_Park promotes a rethinking of the public realm of cities through the design and instigation of parks and other urban green precincts and areas. Effectively, it is a research project where architecture privileges nature over the human-made. Urban green space is vital for a city's overall health and an essential aspect of any forward-thinking planning and revitalization of cities. By prioritizing symbiosis with nature over anthropocentric and haphazard urban sprawl, parks and all urban green areas are paramount in planning for a sustainable and vital future. From this perspective, strategies that tackle head-on pressing issues such as global warming, accelerated urbanization, stressed infrastructure, depleted resources, and many other urgencies are essential. The works presented on the following pages focus on various overlapping issues that could potentially imperil civic life as we know it and offer up intriguing and intelligent solutions and propositions.

A key consideration when discussing the future of parks, and their humanistic designs, stems from some hard lessons learned from the recent and ongoing global pandemic(s). This historical, social experiment has yielded some important lessons, namely the importance of public outdoor spaces, and in particular those spaces within congested and overpopulated cities. The advent of "safety-driven" regulations and the disruption of public programs only heightened awareness of the efficiencies of work-from-home dynamics. They brought to the surface many vital issues, particularly surrounding mental health and what defines our collective wellbeing. City squares, playgrounds, sports fields, vegetable gardens, public parks, and all types of green open territories in the city evidently served to safeguard all essential critical aspects of civic life and thereby prove to be extremely important to many aspects of health equity and collective public welfare.

The projects featured on the following pages have in common a preoccupation with inventing a new sort of resilient urbanism. One that places a sustainable health-oriented method of growth front and center. These unique design approaches make explicit that future enhancements to what constitutes livability and vitality include intelligent responses to many potential environmental threats, be that rising sea levels and flooding, light and noise pollution, or simply access to potable water and other heat-stress-related outcomes.

These projects also put forward various defensive strategies for creating sustainable energy, local food production, tackling waste management issues, and delivering services and goods while being extremely attentive to what makes cities livable and desirable.

By hybridizing traditional architectural programs and typologies with these new repair and reconciliation strategies, these projects promote a multifaceted and inclusive approach targeting what one might call "corrective futures." Scenarios are developed to defend the public realm's overall health.

The paradigm parks are each centered primarily on cultural issues that intersect with aspects of escapism, leisure, and pleasure, using innovation, resilience, and technological advancement as tools. In this context, Paradigm_Park proposals all focus on the possibility of a shape-shifting transient, and continually forming, urbanism that targets a genuinely sustainable future for urban centers.

TIDAL TERRAINS
⊗ LONDON, UK
A Landscape Capable of Dynamic Interaction within a Fluid Context

The site chosen for the project "Tidal Terrains: A Landscape Capable of Dynamic Interaction within a Fluid Context" is the Thames River in the City of London.

Historically, this river was a great place of social exchange and recreation. But by the 1950s it had become unfit for human occupation.
The bombing of the Bazalgette sewers, coupled with a large population, meant that sewage was leaking straight into the river, causing widespread outbreaks of cholera. This moment drastically changed people's relationship with the river and despite the fact that the water quality has since improved, there has been a reluctance to embrace it as the engaging landscape it once was.

Mary Hughes

TIDAL TERRAINS

Climate change experts predict a temperature rise of up to four degrees in the next millennium. This increase will result in a drastic reorganization of our planet as sea levels rise and more extreme weather events, such as hurricanes and tsunamis, disturb our cities. Ninety percent of the world's largest cities are located next to the water. To address increasing population density and different environmental conditions, perhaps we need to start looking at using existing urban water as a place of opportunity to build on with new types of the dynamic landscape able to respond flexibly to changing tidal levels.

The project aims to change this mindset by reestablishing the river as an active place of invention and connection between both sides of London. The proposal incorporates swimming, the agricultural farming of algae, restaurants, and boulevards into a floating-park typology that embraces water and encourages access in order to make it once again a sociable, livable part of the city. Within these programs, the landscape integrates a cycle in which algae, wastewater, and atmospheric CO_2 are converted to energy, food products, and clean water. As such, this means that the dirty water of the Thames River becomes an asset for the production of energy, rather than a commodity to be expensively processed.

Notions such as fluidity, buoyancy, and constant change in relation to the seven-meter tidal height difference of the river are the central driving principles behind the design. Using buoyant concrete elements supported by a series of underwater pistons, parts of the landscape are able to float up or down in neutral buoyant positions with the river height, or artificially close certain air valves to fix them at alternative heights in order to accommodate different programs or more optimal outdoor comfort conditions, such as shielding users from wind or too much sunlight radiation.

Paradigm_Park

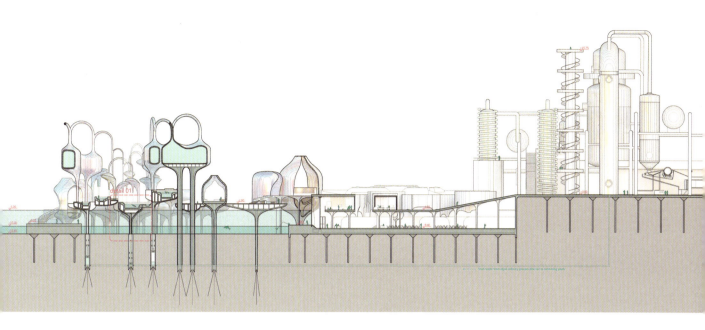

TIDAL TERRAINS

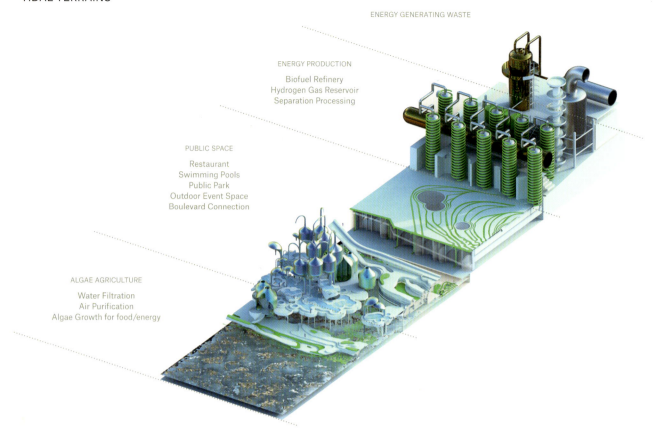

ENERGY GENERATING WASTE

ENERGY PRODUCTION
Biofuel Refinery
Hydrogen Gas Reservoir
Separation Processing

PUBLIC SPACE
Restaurant
Swimming Pools
Public Park
Outdoor Event Space
Boulevard Connection

ALGAE AGRICULTURE
Water Filtration
Air Purification
Algae Growth for food/energy

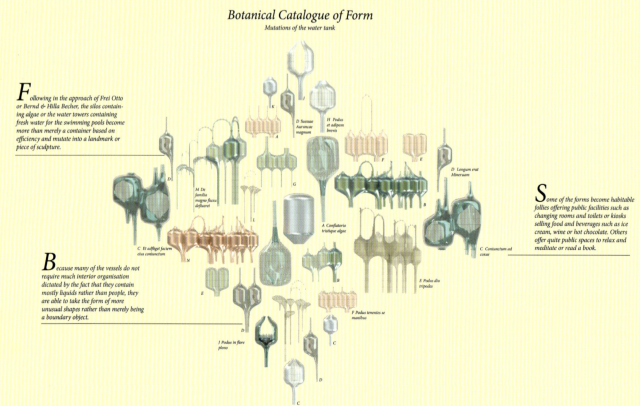

Botanical Catalogue of Form
Mutations of the water tank

*F*ollowing in the approach of Frei Otto or Bernd & Hilla Becher, the silos containing algae or the water towers containing fresh water for the swimming pools become more than merely a container based on efficiency and mutate into a landmark or piece of sculpture.

*B*ecause many of the vessels do not require much interior organisation dictated by the fact that they contain mostly liquids rather than people, they are able to take the form of more unusual shapes rather than merely being a boundary object.

*S*ome of the forms become habitable follies offering public facilities such as changing rooms and toilets or kiosks selling food and beverages such as ice cream, wine or hot chocolate. Others offer quite public spaces to relax and meditate or read a book.

During high and low tides, the landscape assumes naturally buoyant positions. At these times, certain air valves may be opened to enable air to circulate through a series of thin steel pipes and create the sound of a water organ. During mid-tide, the landscape fixes its position at differing heights according to program and environmental requirements by closing the air valves within the pistons. The air pressure within the piston body supports the weight, but because air is no longer circulating freely through the pipes in the structure, the landscape loses its musical properties. The differing height levels transform the swimming area into a series of waterfalls instead of a level, continuous swimming area.

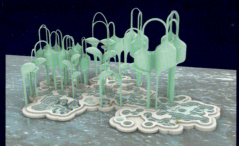
Tide Height : 1.5m

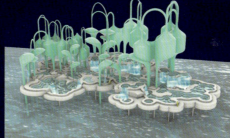
Tide Height : 1.5-5.5m

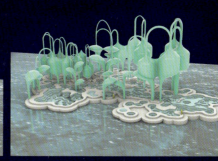
Tide Height : 6m

DOPE_CITY
E-Waste: Recycling as Edutainment

⊗ TURKU, FINLAND

The port of Turku acts as Finland's gateway to the west for trade, tourism, and culture.[1] It is a vital source for the whole region, as it is a central part of the maritime cluster of southwest Finland. Furthermore it strengthens the city's maritime image and is a major attraction factor.

Turku has, in the past, experienced flooding from heavy rains and is naturally concerned about its proximity to the water. With its aim of carbon neutrality by 2029, the city already has a variety of sustainable policies in place: the Kakolanmäki wastewater plant, textile recycling, the heating plant replacing coal with biofuels, a general understanding of the heavy climate impact of meat production, and so forth. Turku has further entered into international cooperation with two cities from around the world to help combat the climate crisis.

Luca Melchiori, Yana Ostapchuk, Shilun Yang

20

Paradigm_Park

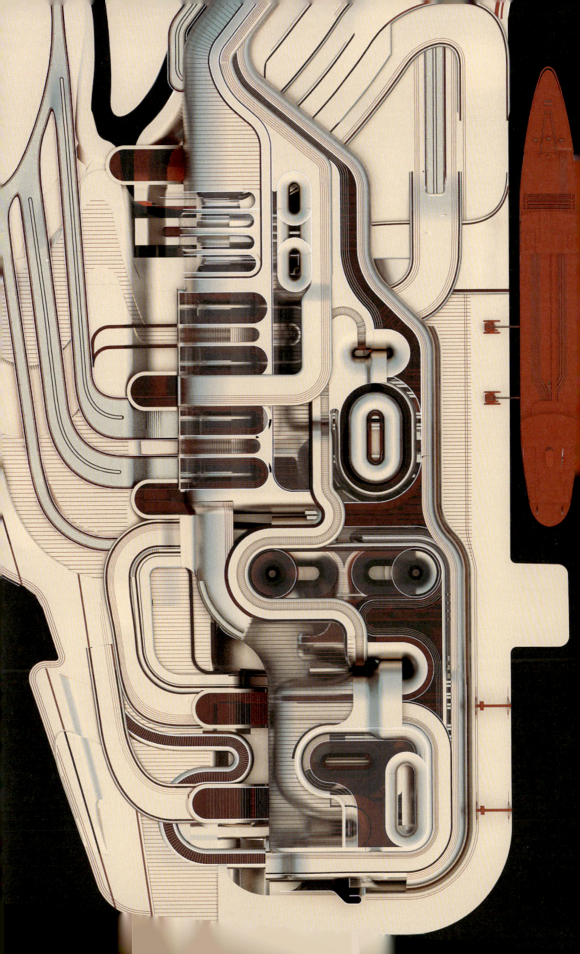

DOPE_CITY

In addition to addressing local issues, Dope_City seeks to take on the growing global problem of e-waste by proposing an innovative recycling plant. The facility is able to transform e-waste into precious raw materials, The separated raw materials will get transported to the main storage spaces, and finally shipped to the industries of Turku or exported worldwide.

The main architectural idea of Dope_City is to bring a certain level of transparency to the industrial processes of recycling e-waste. The project showcases these processes for educational purposes in order to bring attention to a major existing problem. The sorting and recycling procedures become a spectacle themselves, especially when automated and on a large scale. All the different technologies and systems playing together create an intricate choreography.

The site for the project is situated in between the recreational and industrial zone alongside the passenger hub of the harbor, thus creating a hybrid of its surroundings, becoming a 21st century role model for urban and industrial development. The scheme forms a new attraction point in the city, which could become a role model for other cities as it seeks to further develop a societal, economical, and environmental response.

In a contemporary master plan, the transition between the different functions and processes, and the pedestrian access toward and throughout the facility, is paramount. The focus was to resolve the area where these two entities converge and interact with each other. The main recycling plant is placed near the seafront and connected with the harbor, which works as an interface to directly connect the facility with the incoming cargo ships. Besides the recycling factory, the underground square caters for recreational and exhibition events. Along the industrial area, the park helps to attract people to the recycling facility.

DOPE_CITY

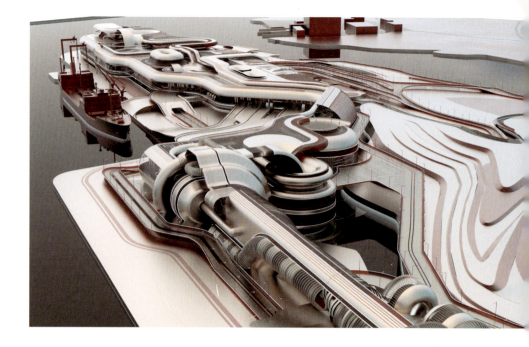

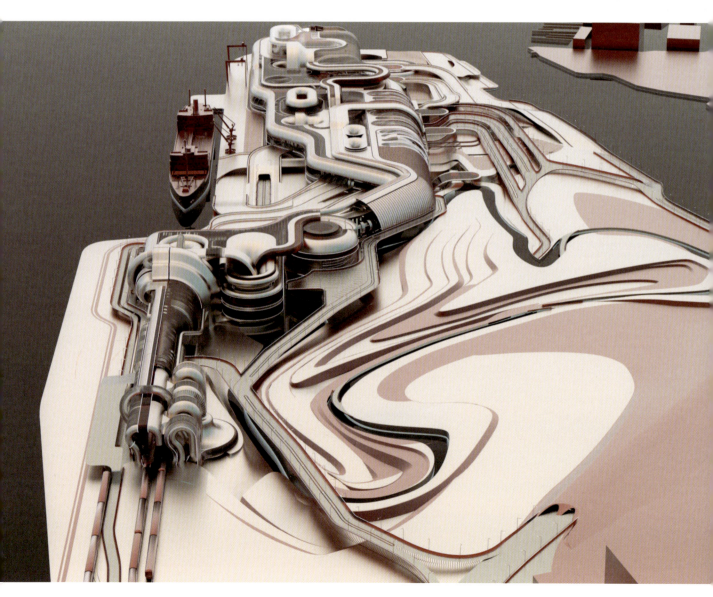

Paradigm_Park

The materiality of the building aims to enhance the visitor's experience without influencing the efficiency of the facility. The machine spaces are indicated by different translucent surfaces. They are composed of frosted-glass panels that reveal the working spaces, but only to a limited degree as to prevent disturbances in these sensitive environments. Translucent parts on the facade of the steel-plated structure help to reveal some elements and spaces inside of the building. Therefore, even from the outside, people can already get a glimpse of some of the recycling processes while walking through the landscape. Through all of this the project brings awareness of ecological and social responsibility toward conserving the environment and its resources.

1   "A Five-Star Service Harbour, Because Time Matters," Port of Turku, June 2, 2021, www.portofturku.fi/en/.

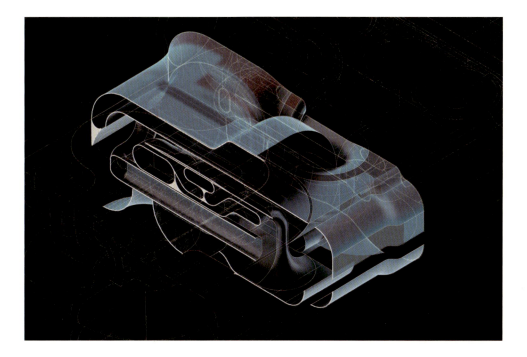

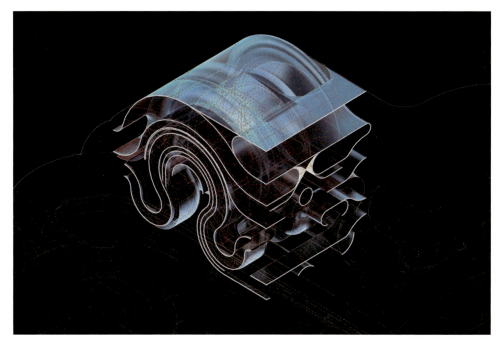

Re: Action

MoMAS
Modern Museum of Audible Space

⊗ NEW YORK CITY, USA

"MoMAS" is envisioned as a network of installation-art galleries and areas for artists to create; proposed as an expansion of the public space around New York City's shoreline, drawing from the rich history of the city's piers connecting the city to the water, so that art may be introduced to a more general audience. Both above-water and underwater level circulation paths bridge the space between Pier 25 and 26, opening up a larger area for both locals and visitors alike to enjoy. Developed to gradually enter the river, the building goes from activation by guests at the shoreline to successively following the ebb and flow of the Hudson at its pier.

Witchaya Jingjit, Emma Sanson, Patricia Tibu

MoMAS

Paradigm_Park

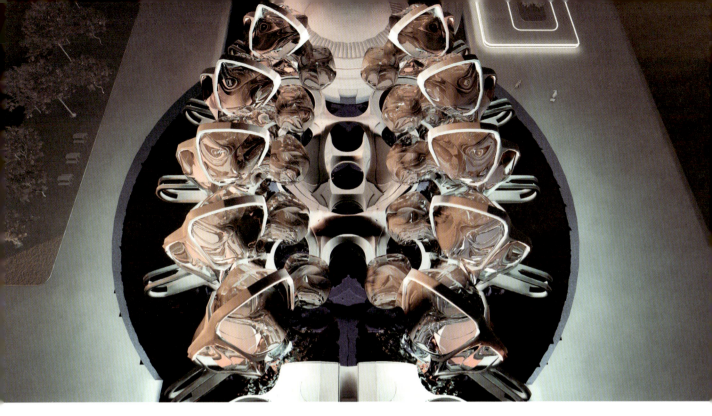

MoMAS

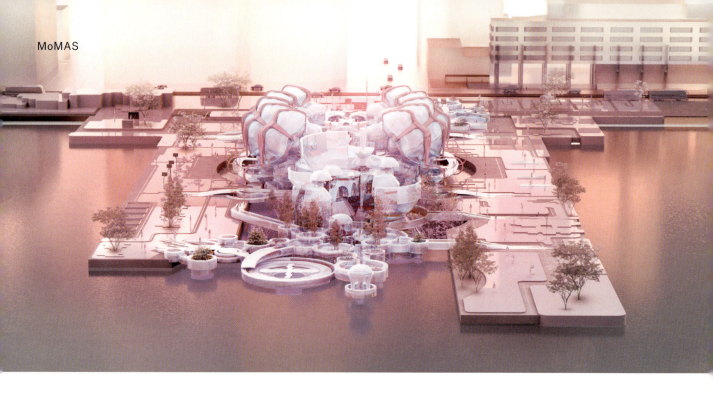

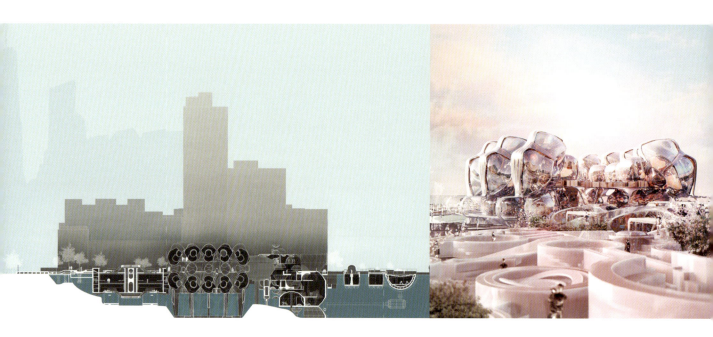

Paradigm_Park

By adding to the shoreline, the Modern Museum of Audible Space expands on New York's limited traffic-free public space. Celebrating the shoreline and its inherent qualities, it opens up an area earlier unavailable to the general public and celebrates it through human creativity and invention. The studios within the building are adaptive to their users through a modular system run on the hydraulic core: the studios can expand, contract and rotate depending on the intentions of the installation being developed. The public pass-through ensures transparency and openness to the public realm while obtaining a strong connection to the neighboring piers. Complete with a performance park at its outermost point, sitting between floating planters and meandering paths, the landscape is segmented into various smaller moments for people, insects, and animals to inhabit.

The space sequences share a strong relationship with the waterscape. They not only make use of the tidal character of the Hudson in order to produce energy and trigger multiple interactive sound systems, but are also sensitive towards the spatial qualities that water immersion affords. The Museum is envisioned as a kinetic building, becoming an instrument of atmosphere next to network-based spaces configured by sound itself. Human occupation becomes a means by which the building changes itself and its immediate environment. The design is aimed at encouraging interaction between visitors and resident artists alike, composing and communicating together without the need for a common language, where sound has become the new medium of both form and interconnection. Adding the distinctive location of the Hudson to the mix, it becomes a space for people to connect to both the water and to each other through sound.

The bigger the variety of occupancy, the more dramatic the changes. A space where the artist not only controls the medium, but also the space itself and an alternate reality where large-scale architectural manipulation is possible through a unique location—the Hudson.

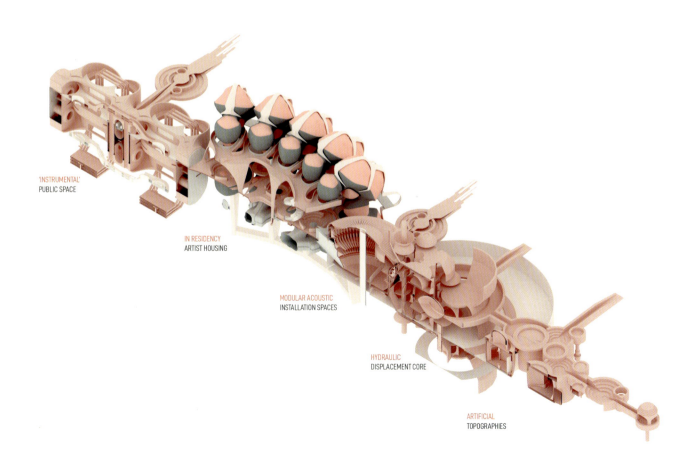

'INSTRUMENTAL' PUBLIC SPACE

IN RESIDENCY ARTIST HOUSING

MODULAR ACOUSTIC INSTALLATION SPACES

HYDRAULIC DISPLACEMENT CORE

ARTIFICIAL TOPOGRAPHIES

FLORAFUTURA
Temple of the Lost Future

⊗ BRUSSELS, BELGIUM

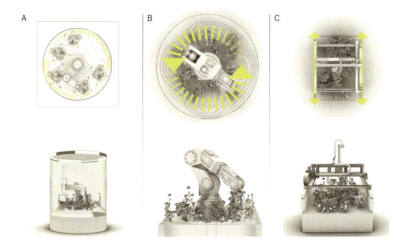

A   B   C

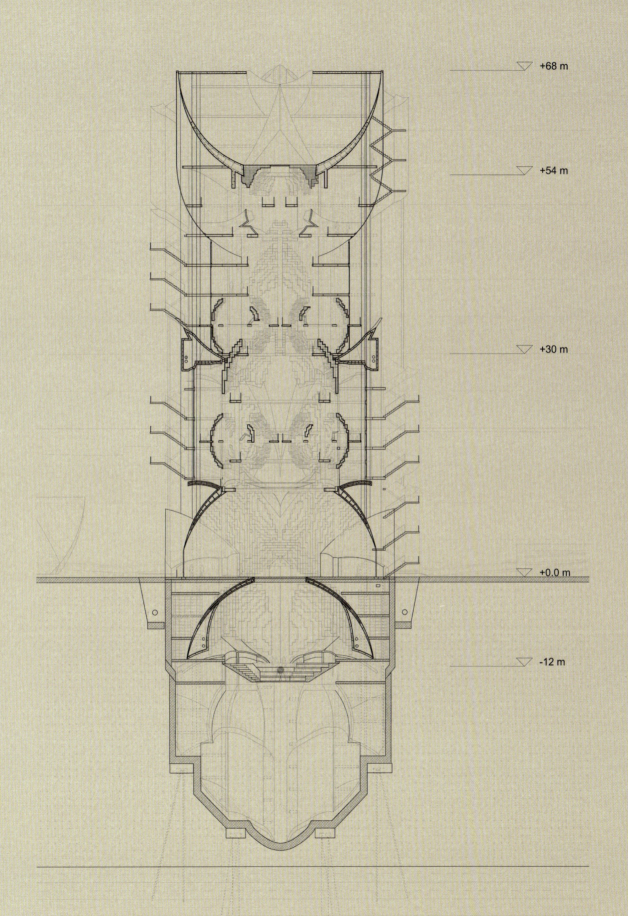

Re: Action　　33

FUTURE FOSSILS
Park of Baroque Objects

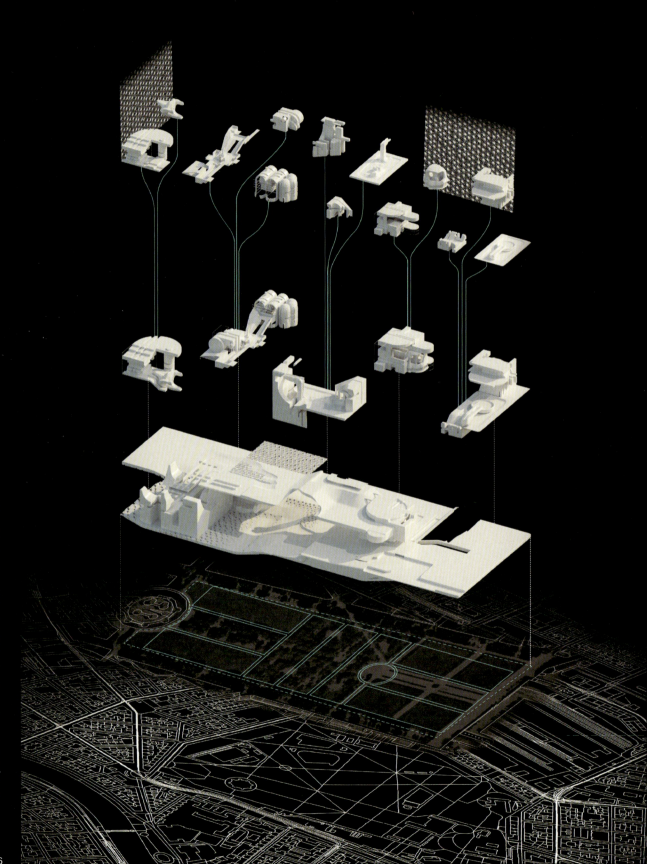

Flakturm_Object   Water_Object / Ground_Object   Conglomerated Object

 +  —Modified→

 +  —Modified→

 + —Modified→

 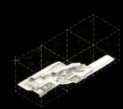

Re: Action

  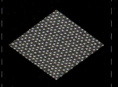 

Water Object　　Water Object　　Water Object　　Flak Tower Object　　Baroque Object　　Ground Object

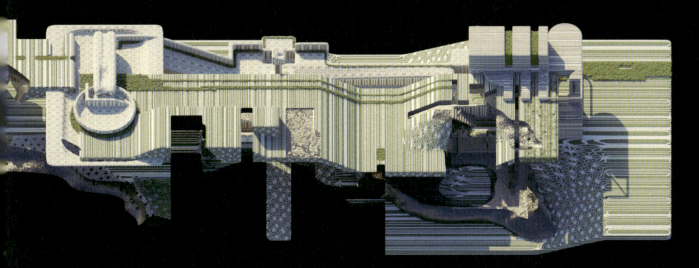

MEDIUS PAEDAGOGICUS
Re-Wilding Augarten

⊗ VIENNA, AUSTRIA

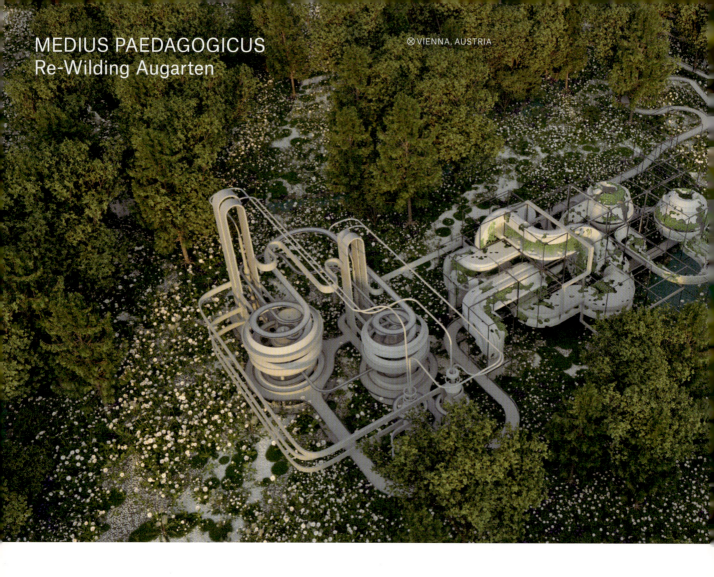

 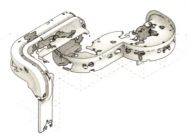 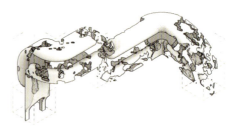

Adham Sinan Hamedaat, Mohamed Abdelhady Omar, Olja Radovanovic

Re: Action

MEDIUS PAEDAGOGICUS

42 Paradigm_Park

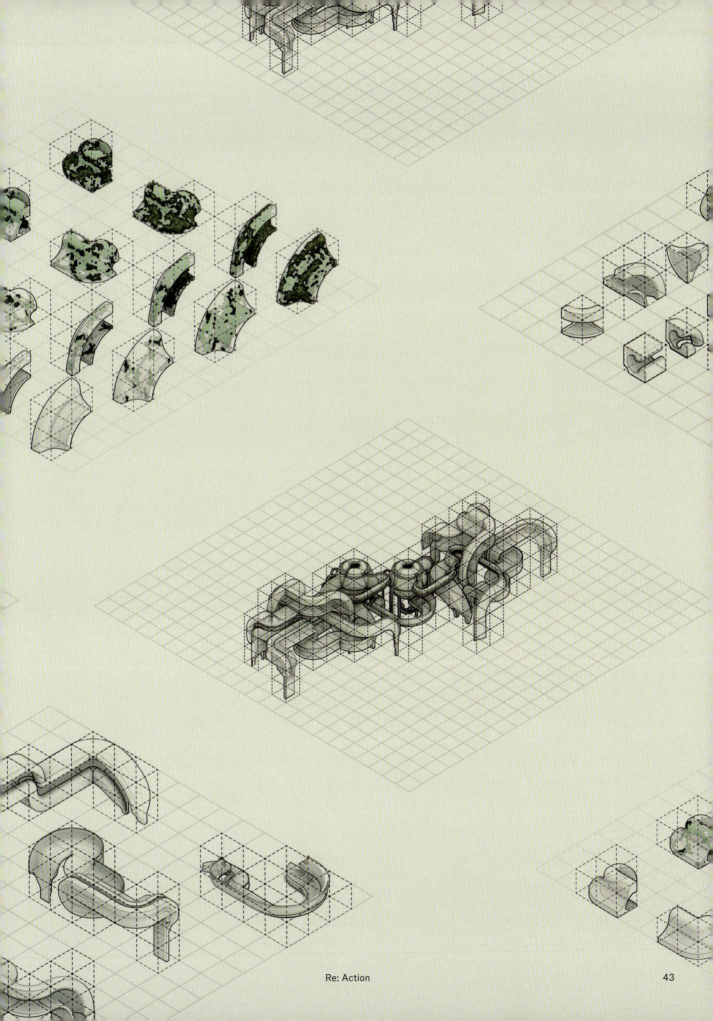
Re: Action

Oceanic_Urbanism: a design research initiative centered on the future of major metropolitan areas and infrastructure located precariously where inhabited lands meet large bodies of water. The past, present, and future of urbanization are all indelibly intertwined with the efficiency and functionality of coastal corridors, waterways, and oceanic trade routes. These locations and territories have been essential to human development, culture, and mass habitation, and by extension are vital to the future of humankind.

Many of the world's largest and most prosperous cities are located in close proximity to, oceans, seas, rivers, lakes, and inlets, thereby making their sustainability and vitality of paramount geopolitical, economic, and cultural importance. While sociological aspects and the urban character of such important locations have been under extreme strain and in a constant state of flux in respect to population growth and resources, today there is an even more urgent need to secure their collective futures as vibrant, globally significant centers.

As one of the most destructive consequences of today's escalating climate crisis, global warming is a game-changing existential threat to waterfront urbanism across the planet. Storm surges and extreme flooding can bring about dramatic population shifts and environmentally instigated mass migrations, so in this regard, Oceanic_Urbanism addresses and attempts to mitigate some of the risks associated with the crisis, rising water levels in particular.

The projects included in the following chapter investigate several innovative ideas, including concepts such as coastal containment and nature-focused preservation strategies. Some design approaches propose new ideas for resilience and architectural ideations to combat extreme weather phenomena and their impact on built and natural environments.

These projects have embraced a spirit of optimism while instigating sound and intelligent strategies for repair and reconciliation as one aspect of a more considerable antidote to the anthropogenic harm caused to the oceanic ecosphere. The proposals put forward some intriguing new typologies for the post-industrial epoch of waterfront infrastructure while responding to the urgency brought about by climate change. They include new modes of sustainable airports, river ports, and seaports, among a roster of possible approaches, while others propose future scenarios that tackle the impacts we face on civic life along water edges. These are all hybrid architectural programs that intertwine new concepts of living, working, and leisure with sophisticated models for oceanic preservation, water mobility, and energy production.

AEROPOLIS
De Stekels Fluctuating City

⊗ SHALLOWS OF DE STEKELS, NETHERLANDS

The "De Stekels Aeropolis," built on the shallows of an area previously known as "Doggerland," is a proposal for a satellite expansion of Schiphol Airport in the North Sea. Building on Amsterdam's innovative relationship with water, it allows for the city's continuing growing, no longer limited by land area or challenged by rising sea levels.

Alejandro Estrella, Elizaveta Karpacheva, Emma Sanson

AEROPOLIS

Oceanic_Urbanism

Driven by the need for interconnectivity, airports have gradually materialized near every major hub in the world. Amsterdam, a city undergoing a population change, is no exception to this phenomena. With Schiphol Airport making the city hyper-connected, it has become a start-up haven; no longer seeing the younger population come and go, but rather settling and establishing themselves into a globalized and flourishing city. However, with this growth comes complications. Schiphol Airport faces expansion challenges due to limited land and noise restrictions, with it being the third busiest airport in Europe and located close to Amsterdam. De Stekels Aeropolis, a floating expansion of Amsterdam and Schiphol, aims to tackle these issues by providing a new, hybrid landscape.

Combining emerging hyperloop and port technology, the new landscape relieves the heavily trafficked port areas of Rotterdam and Amsterdam by becoming a new loading dock for the liquid bulk import and export. Being a new typology of artificial landscape, it brings people closer to the ocean while creating a new marine environment through its geometry and sub-sea topography. Powered by electricity-generating lagoons, Aeropolis is self-sufficient, relying on tidal energy, utilizing its marine position to work with, instead of against, the ocean.

Inspired by water, but built up as a hyper-engineered structure, Aeropolis takes advantage of its unlimited space and the dynamics of the water. Becoming a clustered landscape, growing and diminishing over time, it aggregates naturally with the potential to link and unlink into new islands. With a focus on bio-inspired elements such as pockets, pores and porosity, the sub-water structures aim to become a hybrid landscape, showcasing marine life embracing the new reef material. With the main branch of research being algae and kelp, different microclimates are created throughout Aeropolis to encourage different types of growth. Its location in the North Sea also offers close-range opportunities for research of the sea bed and the surrounding ocean, exploring one of the least explored territories on Earth.

Powered by electricity-generating lagoons, Aeropolis is self-sufficient, relying on tidal energy, utilizing its marine position to work with, instead of against, the ocean.

FUTURE TRACES
Cultural Infrastructure

⊗ ROME, ITALY

"Future Traces" is an exploration into reconfiguring single-purpose transportation infrastructures into hybrid architectures of civic and environmental significance. The proposal is located around Fiumicino Airport on the southwestern outskirts of Rome, where the intervention aims to dissolve the inward-looking nature of today's airport in order to find a more culturally productive coexistence for the infrastructure and its surroundings.

Sarah Agill, Shpend Pashtriku, Raffael Stegfellner

Re: Action

FUTURE TRACES

As it currently stands, the airport is an overly dominant presence within its context; an area of immense historical significance due to its origin as the harbor city of Ancient Rome. Two thousand years prior, the harbor used to be a primary node for commerce and transportation grounded by a thriving community of 60,000 people. Their relationship to water was not only of great economic and political significance, but of a deeply cultural and social one too—as seen through the study of the spaces that used to serve as the civic centers of society: the bathhouses. However, with the fall of Rome, the port was abandoned and over time, due to environmental shifts, became silted; a process where small dust-like sediment settles and fills bodies of water as a result of rock or streambed erosion.

Eventually, due to these centuries-long changing water and terrain conditions, Ostia was buried and protected from the decay of passing time. Many ancient ruins underwent this natural preservation process in and around Fiumicino airport, allowing for the unique opportunity to reintroduce traces of Ancient Roman life within the hermetic architecture of a modern airport. The historical remains become a driver to challenge the mundanity of the architecture and its singularity of use in order to create a more humanistic assemblage of transportational, cultural, and recreational spaces. Simultaneously, the intervention serves as a series of non-intrusive flood protection strategies that could mediate and pace the inevitable flow of water inland, as the entire Fiumicino-Ostia region is increasingly under threat in the face of the drastically rising sea levels.

In order to provide long-term protection of the Fiumicino-Ostia region from the increasing risk of tidal floods, the core of the intervention consists of an intricate water regulation and distribution infrastructure—a gravity-driven system that regulates the tidal flow via water storage basins and push-piston mechanics. Laid out on a concave axis beginning by the shoreline, the system aims to neutralize uncontrolled flooding along the shore through a more controlled absorption of water deep into the landmass infrastructure. The artificial water infrastructure interweaves with the existing airport network, where the continual movement of water becomes a key environmental and programmatic strategy. Ultimately, the water is channeled back into the sea with a significant time-lag through the Ancient Roman harbor, Portus, where it merges with the ancient body of water and begins its final redistribution process, as the flux either reverses and gets released back into the layering of inhabited spaces that line the infrastructure, aiding programmatic functioning, or becomes filtered out further into the branches of the Tiber.

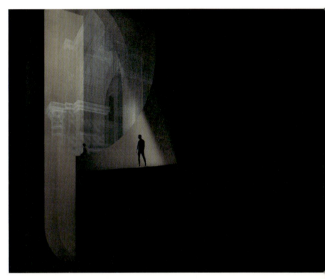
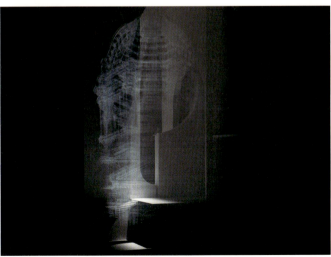
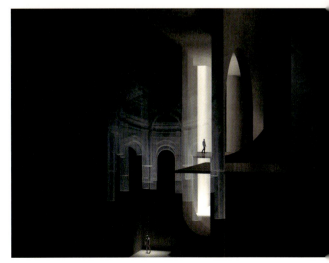

FUTURE TRACES

The circular flow of water, beyond being a regulatory contributor toward the flood protection strategy, is intended as the primary element of cohesion within the proposal, mediating between the infrastructural and the architectural. Along its route, a crafted layering of subterranean and overground spaces form an urban composition that interlinks three primary areas: the remnants of the ancient harbor, the airport's central node and the shoreline. This juxtaposition aims to initiate a dialogue on the preservation of contextual identity in conjunction with the oxygenation of redundant infrastructures in cities. The result becomes an extensive public realm infused with cultural enclaves that resurface what once was so integral to Roman society and its civic life: auditoria, forums and bathhouses. The spaces operate in complete synchronicity with one another, across different gradients of temperature, light, and density, while maintaining the primary function of the transportation hub they lie within, in doing so redefining the airport of the future, not through the optimization of its technology or restructuring it based on a particular transportation medium that will eventually be overridden by time and technological evolution, but through the humanistic value of its spaces and the strengthening of its ties to the context it lies within.

The intervention also stems from a site-specific issue of contextual disconnection and a lack of civic programs. Even though Fiumicino Airport lies right beside one of the most significant ancient sites in the region, a meaningful connection between the two has not yet been defined. On the contrary, the primary infrastructure that enables access to the airport from the City of Rome is a physical obstruction that prevents even the mere acknowledgment of the ruins' existence. At the same time, Ostia's own link to its heritage remains blurred by the dearth of public spheres and cultural programs, further enhanced by the prevalence of industrial sites across the city. Hence, the proposed master plan aims to dissolve the inward-looking nature of the airport by finding a more sustainable, culturally productive coexistence with its surroundings—highlighting the region's dense history, creating public realms that could allow for an open interaction with it, and establishing landscape-integrated low-energy flood protection measures that could protect it.

In order to provide long-term protection of the Fiumicino-Ostia region from the increasing risk of tidal floods, the core of the intervention consists of an intricate water regulation and distribution infrastructure—a gravity-driven system that regulates the tidal flow via water storage basins and push-piston mechanics.

SIAM'S TRASH ABSORBER
The Future of Waste Handling
— Renewing the Thai Floating City

⊗ BANGKOK, THAILAND

"Siam's Trash Absorber" aims to tackle Thailand's growing waste problem and worsening flood situation caused as a direct result of climate change and increasing population growth. In order to do this, the architectural design and program is intended to protect and restore the Chao Phraya estuary and stop sea waste. Primarily this happens by turning garbage into a construction material that is then used to create the floating city. Its form and the notion to revive the currently fading culture of living on water, is inspired by traditional Thai cultures, art, and vernacular architecture.

Witchaya Jingjit

SIAM'S TRASH ABSORBER

A key point of the project is to reconsider waste management within highly urbanized areas that are often affected by intensive and harsh flooding, and contribute toward creating a waste disposal system that can help and respond to flooding by being able to manage waste more effectively. An alternative design strategy is proposed: a floating city.

By absorbing waste, the project aims to clean the river and convert it into construction material for the floating city. It is also designed to rescue people from flooding. During the first phase of the system, waste from the river is sucked through AI waste filters and sent to other zones, such as biodegradation for agriculture, waste to energy, or wastewater treatment for filtration. In the floating city prototype, plastic waste is recycled into a lightweight material that connects the elements and zones together. Components along the river include pods used for transport and living, synced with the entire area. In the event of a flood alert, for example, pods can help people get from low-risk areas to safety while at the same time absorbing the waste and transferring it to the main system. Controlling the balance of risks is based on the changing environment.

As part of the project, a symbol will be created through architecture and space which people in the community will be able to feel and remember. In this way, it serves as a social space where people can share experiences, learn, and create through the creation of a traditional Thai social ecosystem. The design is aimed to be continually built upon and expanded. Its aim is to tell its history and purpose through a layout that corresponds to the ancient way of life. It celebrates different aspects of water and engages with Thai water culture with advanced technology and infrastructure. By creating a new role for architecture to assist humans in surviving, preserving, and restoring our environment, the project aims to remind us of the problem. A key aspect of the project is the combination of technology and cultural preservation to create an ecosystem that allows Thais to enjoy living in the city again in a more sustainable and future-oriented manner.

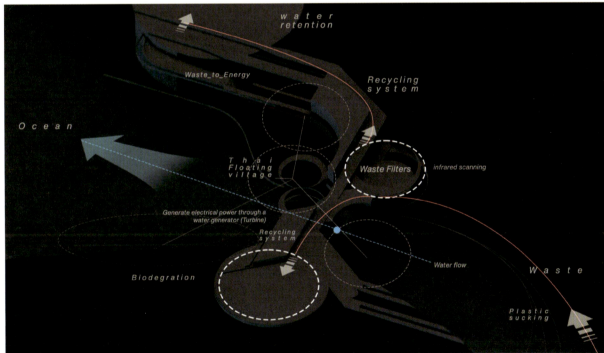

SIAM'S TRASH ABSORBER

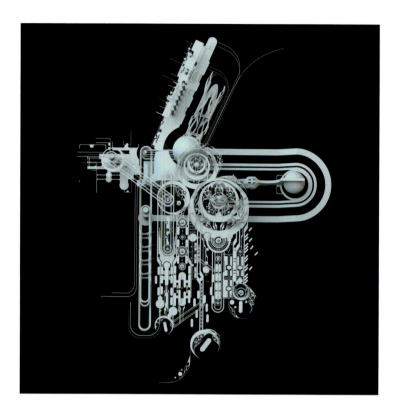

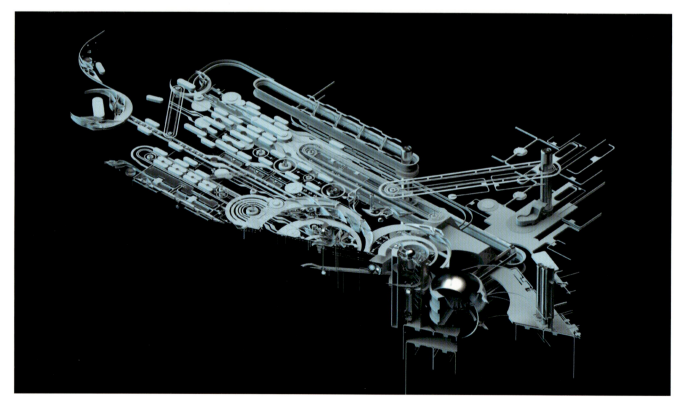

Oceanic_Urbanism

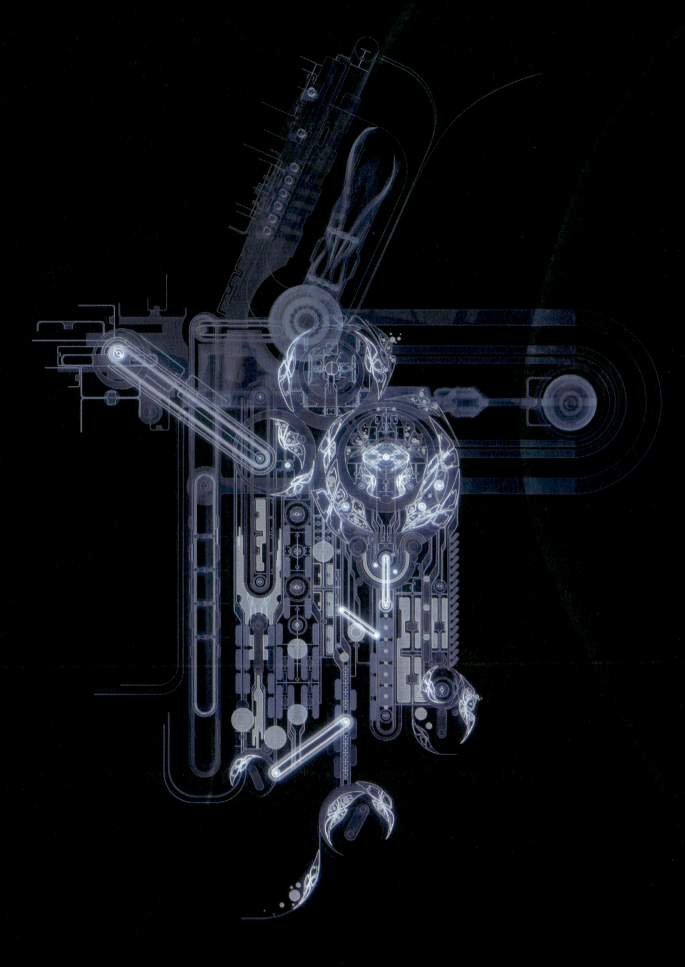

Re: Action

RE-EDGE CITY
Miami 2.0

⊗ MIAMI, USA

Jonghoon Kim

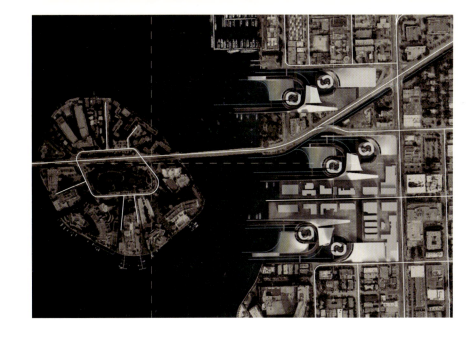

Re: Action

65

RE-EDGE CITY

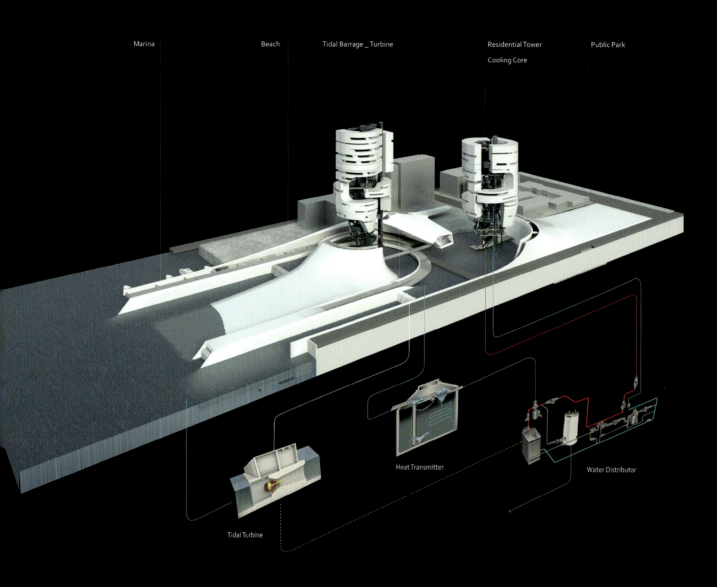

Marina Beach Tidal Barrage _ Turbine Residential Tower / Cooling Core Public Park

Tidal Turbine Heat Transmitter Water Distributor

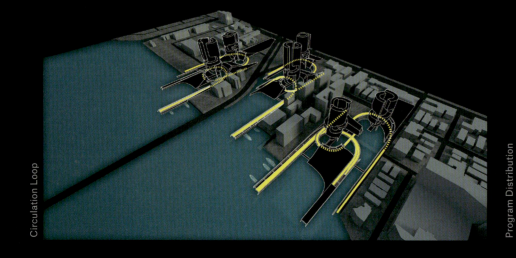

Circulation Loop

Program Distribution

Oceanic_Urbanism

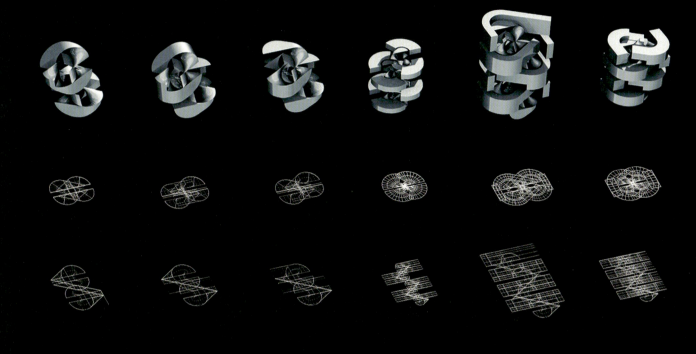

Energy Strategy

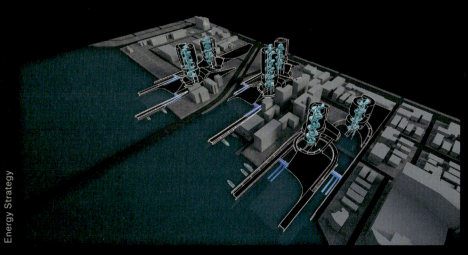

HYPERPORT

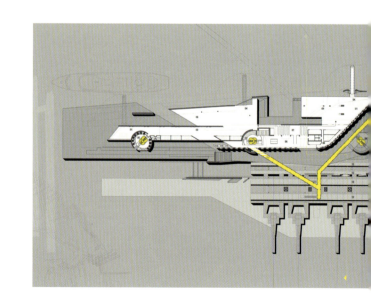

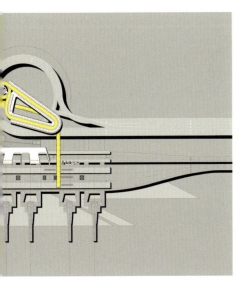

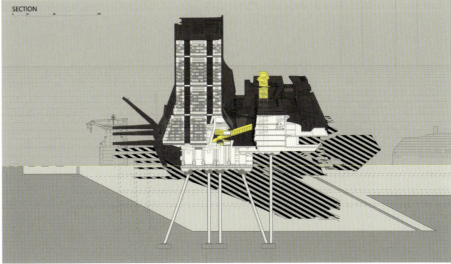

Re: Action

OFFSHORE INFLUX
Renewable Energy Power Plant

⊗ LOFOTEN, NORWAY

Luca Melchiori, Barbara Schickermüller

Oceanic_Urbanism

OFFSHORE INFLUX

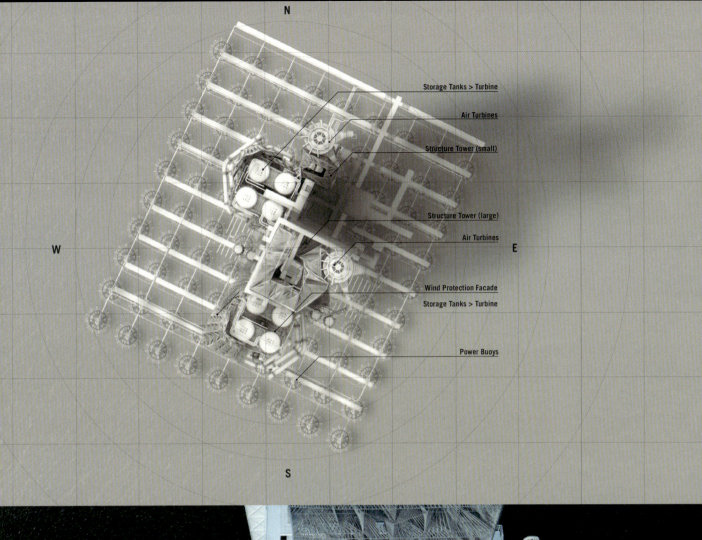

03

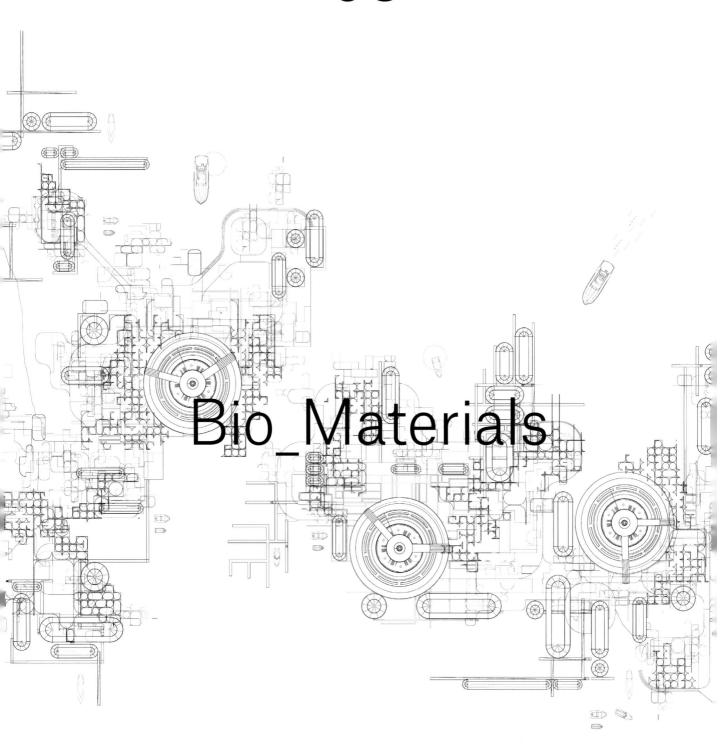

Bio_Materials

One key driver for the immediate future of architectural innovation is the science, technology, and conceptual uses of new materials. Of particular importance, materials of the near future will need to be environmentally sustainable with respect to strategies for their development, methods of production, use and application, as well as lifecycle. Bio_Materials, in particular, are vital protagonists in the quest for such future-looking materials for building. The following pages highlight projects that target innovation through the inclusion of new and cutting-edge materials and construction processes that embrace creative approaches to fabrication responding to environmental concerns and issues.

As global greenhouse emissions reach record highs in the early decades of this century, the urgent call to decarbonize the energy and construction sectors also requires bold and unorthodox architectural responses as part of the equation. It is true that the buildings, and construction industry at large, account for an alarmingly large share of global energy demands through embodied carbon as well as carbon emissions through building use and occupancy. Unsustainable and unrenewable building materials are strongly associated with high energy consumption, waste generation, indoor and outdoor pollution, and a highly polluting lifecycle of buildings. Furthermore, the harmful effects of off-gassing and toxins released from older buildings, and their effects on people's health, are dire. The mismanagement and misunderstanding of nature and the associated economics of material are prompting a transition to new sustainable and natural, renewable materials for building.

Several innovative projects incorporate new and cutting-edge materials on the following pages. Some projects utilize 3D-printed ice structures, recycled charcoal, and timber tectonics, while others conceive of buildings in clay and silt and other works utilize biophilic and biodegradable natural materials such as mycelium and bacteria. Moreover, ideas such as generating building parts from converted CO_2 emissions or algae biomass yield powerful new architectural forms and programs. The concepts and implementation strategies that follow open up untold opportunities for building design centered on environmentally logical and sustainable building-material logic. At the same time, these ideas serve to push the discipline of architecture into the near future with genuinely innovative design strategies and possibilities. In summation, the following design processes are driven by an ambition to unify the realms of design, materials, and technological research into a creative, diverse, and ecologically invaluable architectural worldview.

DESERTED PLAINS
New Agricultural Typologies
in Times of a Climate Crisis

⊗ GRAND VALLEY, USA

Situated in Grand Valley, Colorado, "Deserted Plains" deals with new adaptive agriculture typologies fit for a more sustainable crop production in the wake of an imminent climate crisis. The work further explores how such a technology-driven intervention can be used to reinvigorate the area on an urban scale.

Tilman Fabini, Oliver Hamedinger, Raffael Stegfellner

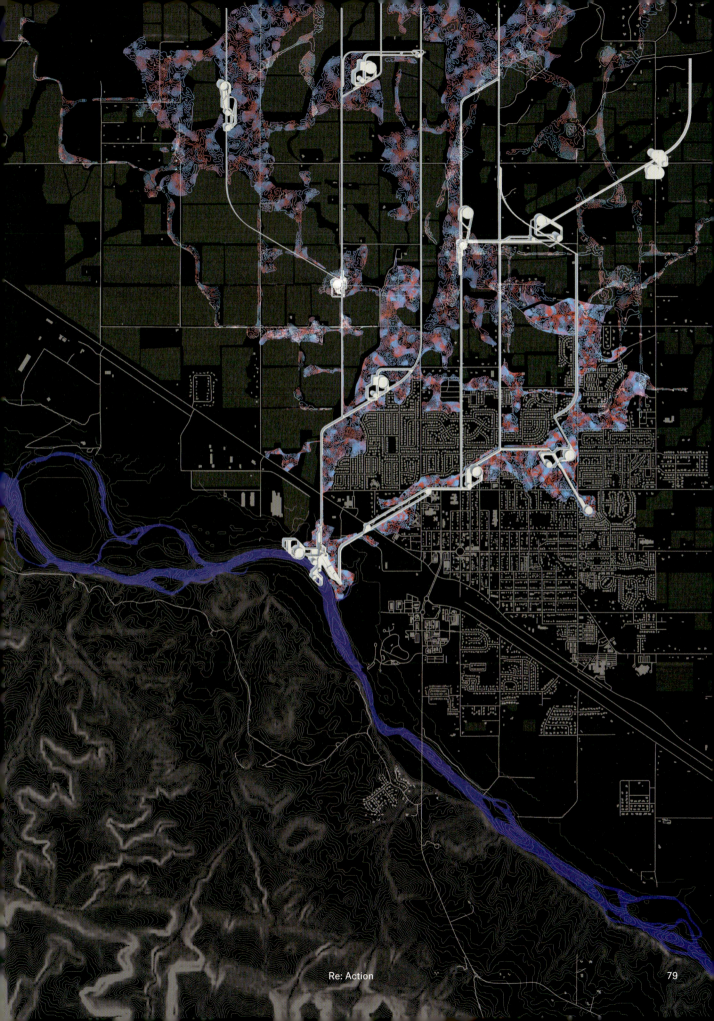
Re: Action

DESERTED PLAINS

The extreme environmental problems of Grand Valley are symptomatic of a larger problem that all of the US Southwest is facing. Rising temperatures and declining precipitation are leading to massive ecological, economic and social implications. Ecologically, a particularly troubling consequence of the changing climate is its effects on the agricultural industry. In order to sustain the immense crop productivity in these areas, farms are relying heavily on dangerous monocultural practices, excessive fertilization, and artificial irrigation. Annually, up to 75% of the Colorado River stream is used for plant irrigation.[1] The excessive crop tempering is also responsible for rising salinization within the remaining fresh water resources. Mineralized fertilizer wastes, as well as salt being washed out from the bedrock due to artificial water flows of irrigation, are both causing these salination spikes. Tackling a more sustainable mode of crop production alongside these circumstances, therefore, must include the possibility of using water resources more efficiently, creating less saline waste, and offering opportunities to grow a diverse range of plants simultaneously. Taking such comprehensive measures is not only necessary on an ecological level, but is needed in order to reinvigorate many economically neglected regions of agricultural production in the US Southwest.

In order to provide solutions on an ecological and civic level, Deserted Plains proposes a new form of agricultural urbanism: A hybrid city canvas, acting as a megastructure and not as individual parts, that reshapes and defines civic, agricultural, and infrastructure programs for a symbiosis of production and consumption. The project ultimately establishes a new agricultural urbanism in which humans, plants, machines, and microorganisms coexist as newly defined bio-citizens. By inhabiting the previously unused perimeter between residential and industrial areas, the intervention aims to revive neglected realms and creates new types of public spaces through a stratified landscape. The layered composition consists of four main components: water processing facilities, hydroponic farming, mycelium-based biodiversity zones, and civic routes. The technological programs within this development aim to provide a framework for agricultural production that simultaneously cleans the water in the present and saves water for the future. Biodiversity and civic zones are intertwined with the functional infrastructure to provide space for the spontaneous appropriation of the space for human and non-human adaption.

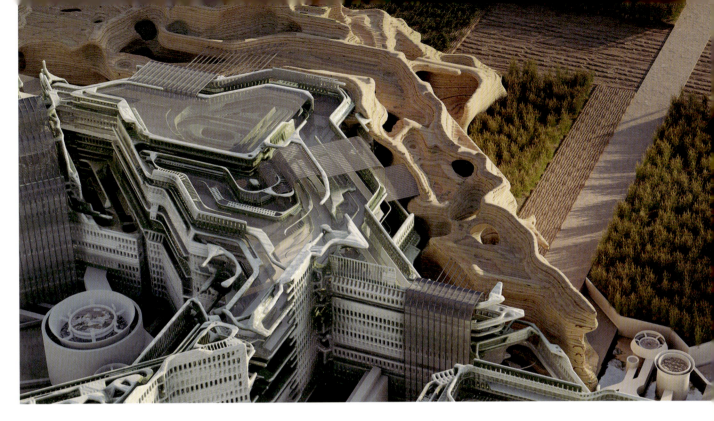

Re: Action

Current strategies of tackling water shortages, as well as salinization, are consistently handled separately. In the future, an interconnected system of desalination and hydroponics could provide a more comprehensive solution to these interconnected issues. While speculative on a superficial level, Deserted Plains is grounded in reality as it takes current prototypical technologies of hydroponic desalination farming and reimagines the architectural potential of this technology on an urban scale. Both the architecture and the technological solution of the project rely on the concept of a closed-loop system. Resources are conserved through a circular strategy, in which waste products are constantly reused in other sections of the workflow. By reintroducing desalination outputs as fertilizers within the hydroponic system, water is saved and waste is reduced. The closed loop system can adjust to future changes in salination through the incorporation of additional aquacultures. The structural framework that houses the infrastructure is also autonomous within its expansion. The mycelium structure uses the agricultural waste of its surrounding as a base to create a building material that is extremely low in embodied carbon. The continual construction uses 3D printing technology which is computationally guided in its expansion. The existing socio-environmental conditions are iteratively translated into computational data streams that guide the architectural articulations into an anticipatory system.

The new agricultural interventions create a scheme that is both technologically functional and urbanistically reinvigorating. This ecocentric coexistence of human and non-human agencies is the primary strategy for a long-term, sustainable urban future.

1   Alex Hager and Luke Runyon."Colorado River water managers face federal call for unprecedented cuts." June 23, 2022. https://cronkitenews.azpbs.org/2022/06/23/colorado-river-water-managers-face-federal-cuts/

The new agricultural interventions create a scheme that is both technologically functional and urbanistically reinvigorating. This ecocentric coexistence of human and non-human agencies is the primary strategy for a long-term, sustainable urban future.

TRACES OF GLOBAL WARMING

⊗ NEW YORK CITY, USA

The core incentive of "Traces of Global Warming" is to juxtapose current theory and political and cultural discourse with the unintended and unexpected through the speculation of ideas and spaces.

The project is outlined through experimentation of form and illustration to help narrate a story of an architectural discourse that hypothesizes a transformation of material and circular strategy. It seeks not only to bring awareness to the obvious impacts of global warming, its impending presence, and those obscured by its inevitability and sheer scale but also to reconcile the environmental damage that has occurred. It attempts this by using methods of bio-fabrication of materials sourced within a certain proximity to the construction site, highlighted as traces of climate change that are residues of the direct impact of the Earth's warming temperatures.

Jade Bailey

Re: Action

TRACES OF GLOBAL WARMING

Current discussions revolve around a dark ecology,[1] a "search for data," a movement that will become our reckoning. As a result, the debate has moved away from systems that use nature and ecology to improve human quality of life, whilst appeasing our capitalist conscience, toward sustainable technologies that help us find the murky middle ground for coexistence between humans and non-humans.

The conceptual design project explores these states of flux, interaction, and process. It aims to take on these qualities of dark ecology by analyzing traces of global warming and using them as a design tool and fabrication method. Taking New York City as the given site location, global warming has caused an increase in flooding and tropical hurricanes. Because of the sea level rise and change in atmospheric conditions, these events are happening more frequently and creating more devastation, leaving behind debris: cultural, economic, social, financial, and immediate physical entities. The project aims to use the physical byproducts, the sedimentation, as a building material, advocating a procedure that can reduce waste production and minimize CO_2 emissions directly connected to the construction industry.

Produced utilizing bio-fabrication, where bacteria are used as the binding material, and the setting process is conducted at room temperature over a couple of days—the process of bio-element manufacture will take place within the building, from collecting to cleaning to sorting, conditioning and fabricating. Outlined within the project are three main material composites that will primarily be harvested: charcoal and timber, clay and silt, and reused concrete from elements removed from the silos. These materials each have defining qualities that relate to how they will be used and function as building components; however, to explore moments of transmogrification, the building houses space for the materials to be applied in unintended configurations and layering.

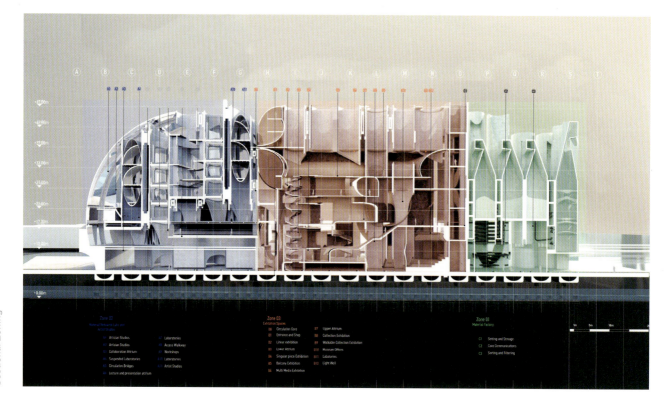

Sectional Zoning

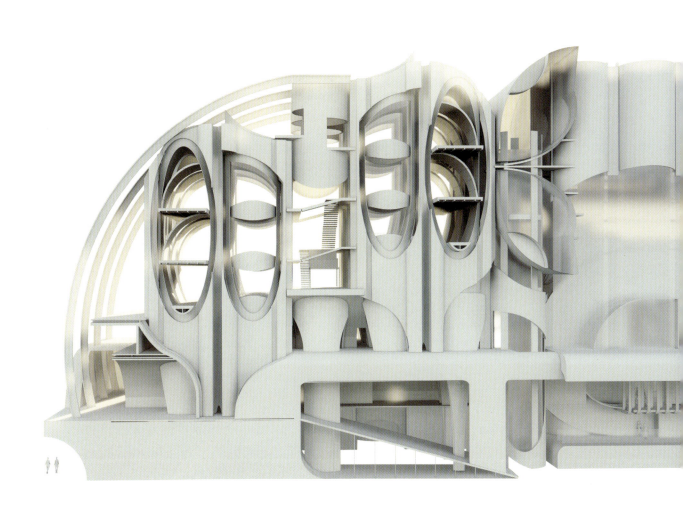

TRACES OF GLOBAL WARMING

Material Archive and Museum

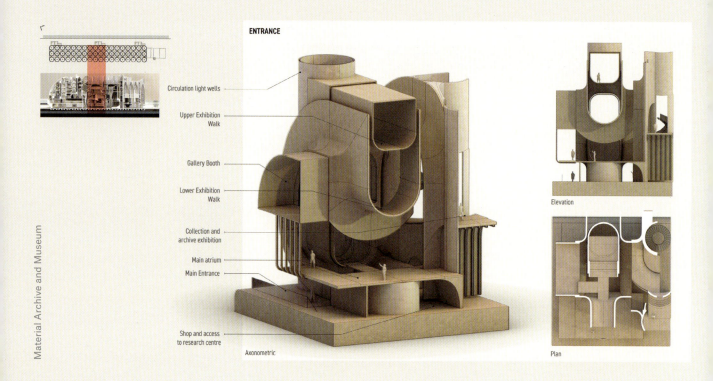

Material Research and Studios

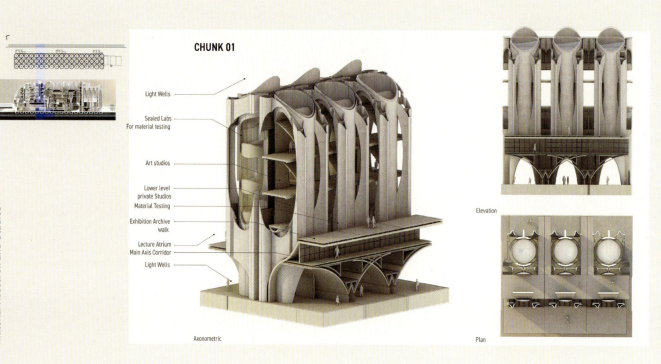

88 Bio_Materials

Inspired by Donna Haraway's "Terrapolis" in *Staying with the Trouble*,[2] the design envisages a way to consider multiple species, dirty materials, and in-between spaces as a way of making sense of the present and de-emphasizing human exceptionalism. The architectural proposal incorporates the production of the building material itself as a material research center in which artists and scientists may collaborate, in addition to an exhibition space that showcases their experiments and developments as an exhibition archive. The building will evolve into a solution-solving center for ecological design as the science and art practiced within intertwines into interdisciplinary states. In doing so, it creates a new cultural experience of art and research that is relevant and engaging. The building itself is a testing ground for material development and spatial exploration that hones in on non-human centricity. This is illustrated through the amount of excess material that houses space for New York City's sub-natures.

1   Timothy Morton, *Dark Ecology: For a Logic of Future Coexistence* (New York: Columbia University Press, 2016).
2   Donna Haraway, *Staying with the Trouble* (Durham/London: Duke University Press, 2016).

"Traces of Global Warming" uses the "traces" of climate change, specifically related to the site context, to enhance ecological responsibility with the intent of advocating and embracing a different understanding of what sustainable design has to offer. It is no longer tied to the strict conditions of human space, instead assuming trial and error, erosion, decay, re-growth, and temporality.
In essence, the architecture becomes a physical manifestation of a museum, illustrating a materiality derived from the context and suggestiveness of global climate change.

PROTOCELL
Building from CO_2

"Protocell" is a project for domestic living that superimposes the efficiency of prefabricated structures with the flexibility of custom design and adaptable space. The "Protocell" system gives every new owner an opportunity to develop from water and CO_2 their own fully customized house in a freely chosen plot, hence the location of the project is abstract and not defined. The lack of specific location characteristics allows the project to focus on global problems and needs without overlooking local conditions.

Monika Kalinowska, Dennis Karandiuk

Re: Action

PROTOCELL

Bio_Materials

One of the main drivers for the project is the constantly deteriorating condition of the global climate. The amount of CO₂ pollution has dramatically increased in recent years, with a substantial detriment to the planet's climate. On May 13, 2019, the carbon dioxide level hit a historic high."The built environment generates 40% of annual global CO₂ emissions. Of those total emissions, building operations are responsible for 27% annually, while building and infrastructure materials and construction (typically referred to as embodied carbon) are responsible for an additional 13% annually."[1] Therefore, the Protocell project's main objective and purpose is to find a way of transforming the problem, harmful emissions, into a solution, and use CO₂ pollution as the new building construction material.

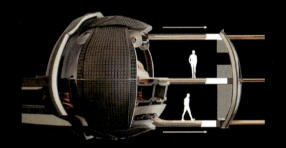

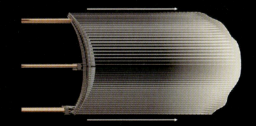

PROTOCELL

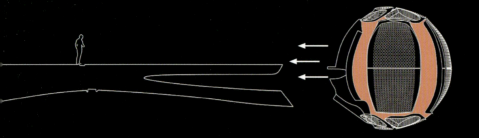

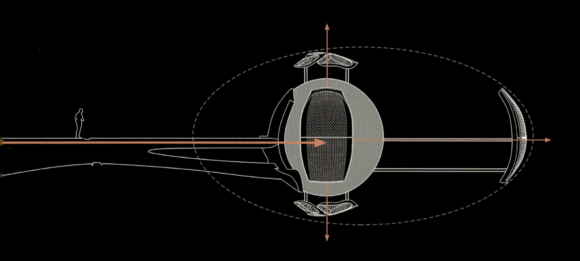

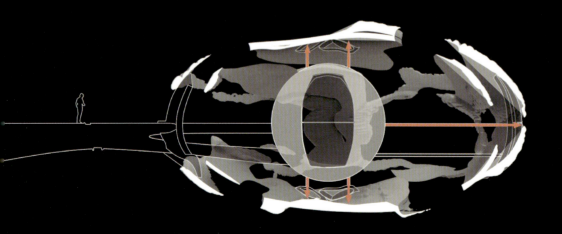

Bio_Materials

The project goal is to envision a solution for architecture on the edge between natural processes and future-oriented technologies, to propose a flexible and efficient way of producing inhabitable, fully adaptable structures. With the use of contemporary technologies, the project superimposes the efficiency of prefabricated modules with the flexibility of custom design and adaptable space.

Programmatically, the project proposes an adaptable dynamic system capable of creating any configuration of the premises required for a specific area. From the perspective of technologies, the project is trying to push the idea of prefabrication to its limits by fully basing the primary system of the project on modular and kinetic elements. As a result, the project proposes an architectural solution where efficiency comes from the technological mechanism and flexibility is based on natural, biological processes.

The primary building-material concept of Protocell ensures a sustainable urban future. By using genome-modified yeast to "convert carbon dioxide gas to carbonates for building materials,"[2] the project envisions a game-changing approach for the building industry on a fundamental level. Instead of using traditional building materials with their inevitable CO_2 emissions in the production stage, we are capable of inverting this process and mitigating the building sector's CO_2 pollution that has been growing exponentially in recent years.

1   "Why the Building Sector?," Architecture 2030, accessed December 22, 2022, www.architecture2030.org/why-the-building-sector/.
2   "Using Yeast to Convert Carbon Dioxide Gas to Carbonates For Building Materials," MicrobeWiki, accessed December 22, 2022, https://microbewiki.kenyon.edu/index.php/User:Using_Yeast_to_Convert_Carbon_Dioxide_Gas_to_Carbonates_For_Building_Materials.

PHASE-TRANSITION
Temporary Ice Arena

⊗ CORTINA D'AMPEZZO, ITALY

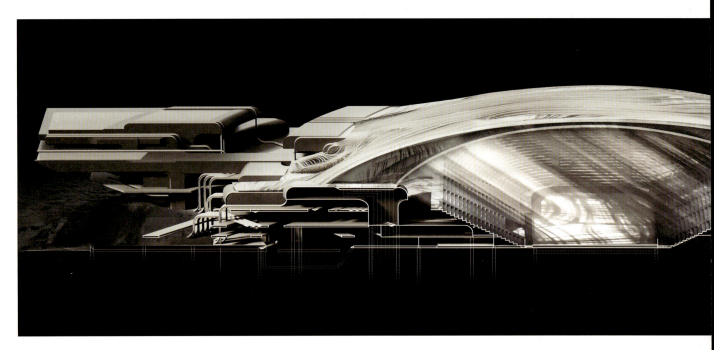

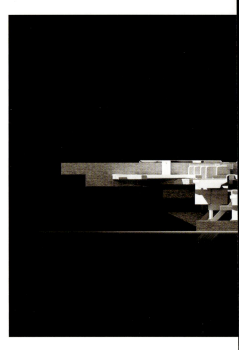

Alejandro Estrella, Monika Kalinowska, Dennis Karandiuk

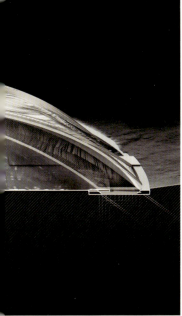

Re: Action

PHASE-TRANSITION

98 Bio_Materials

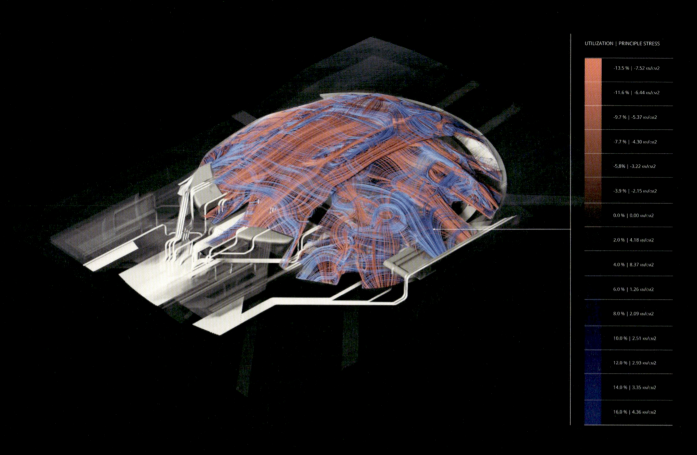

PHASE TRANSITION | DOME

ICE FORMATION

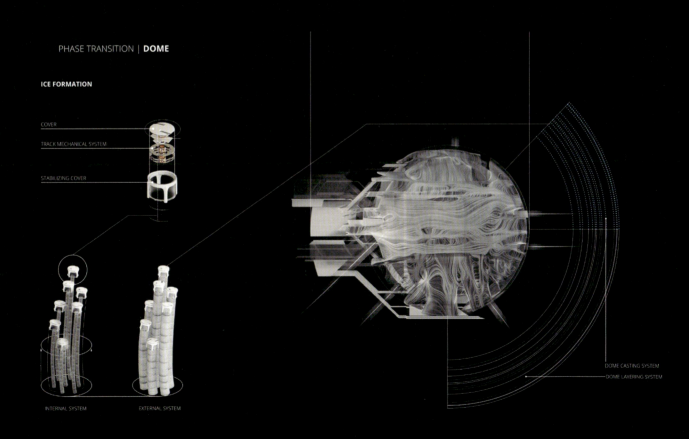

HEATHROW
Future3500_Nature 2.0

⊗ HEATHROW, UK

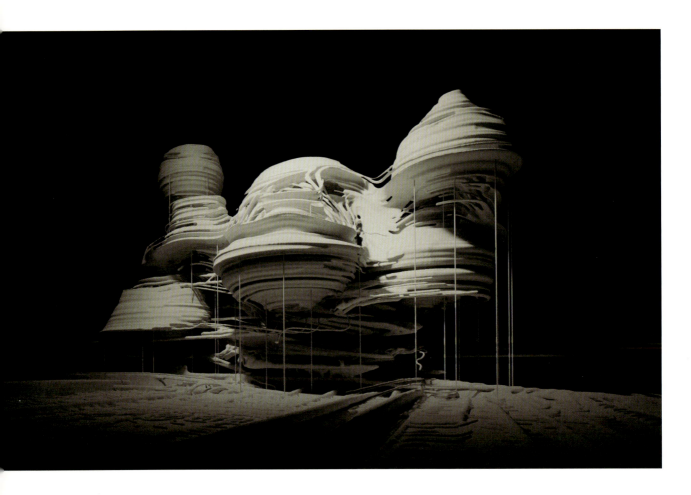

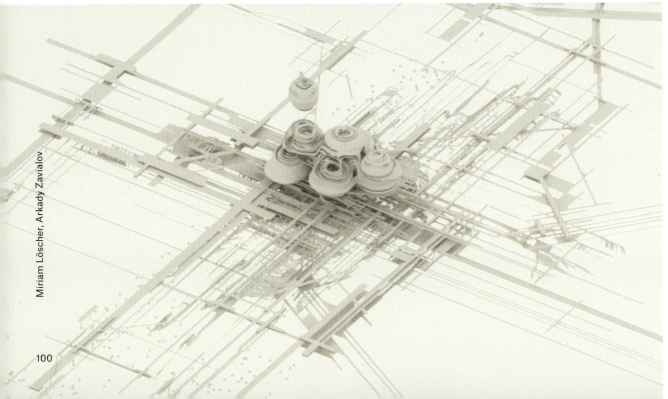

Miriam Löscher, Arkady Zavialov

RECRETE PARK
Deconstructing Flak Tower

⊗ VIENNA, AUSTRIA

Louis Braunger, David Kipp, Gaowei Zhou

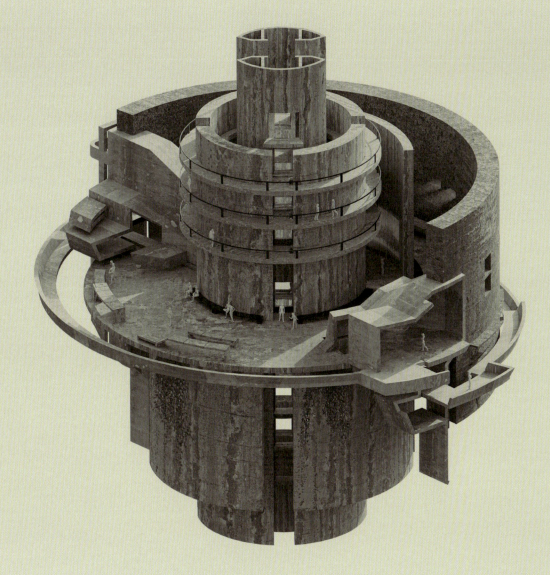

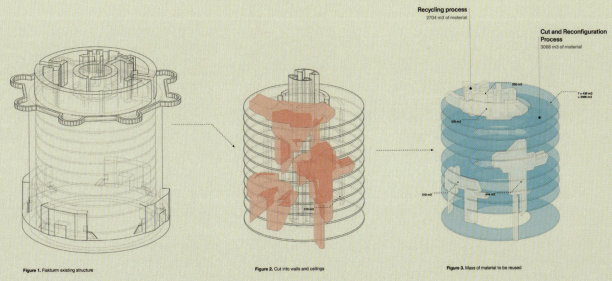

Figure 1. Flakturm existing structure
Figure 2. Cut into walls and ceilings
Figure 3. Mass of material to be reused

Recycling process
2704 m3 of material

Cut and Reconfiguration Process
3066 m3 of material

Re: Action

Re: Action

SYMBIOTIC BLOOMS
Renewable Energy Power Plant

⊗ LAKE ATITLAN, GUATEMALA

Sarah Agill, David Kipp, Sharon Sarfati, Shpend Pashtriku

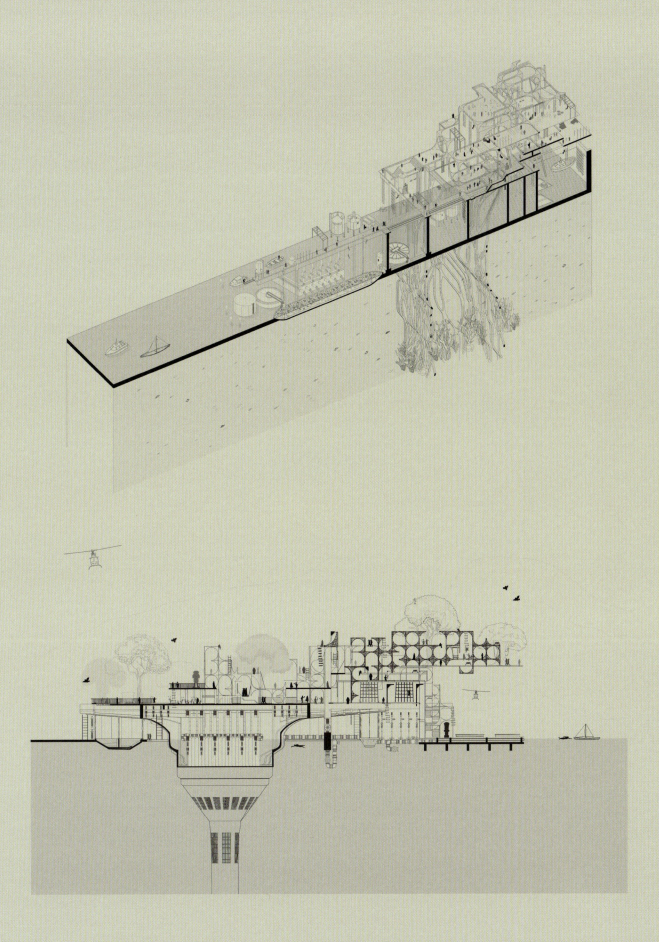

04

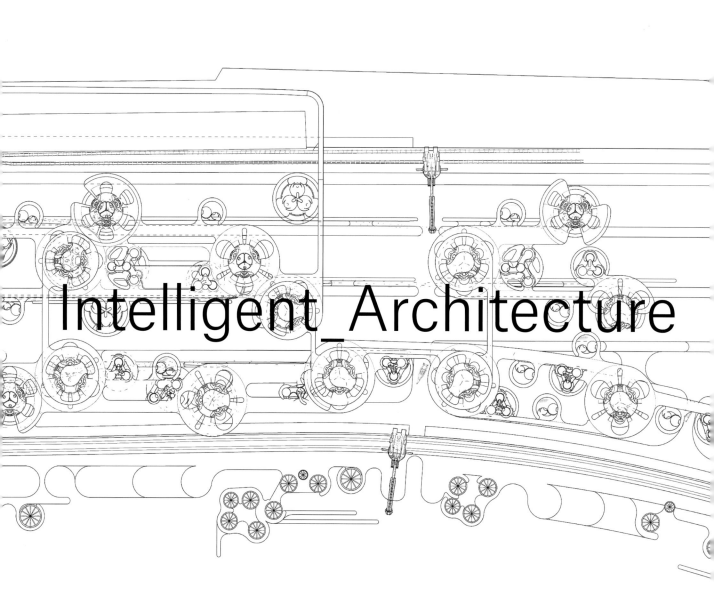

Intelligent_Architecture

The notion of "intelligence" has gained wide popularity in 21st-century discourse, allowing countless meanings and connotations as it infiltrates different disciplines and relates to diverse contexts. In most cases, it opposes a primitive, unsophisticated, non-responsive, and non-adaptable way of interacting with the surrounding environment. On the contrary, it contains an advanced, computationally enhanced, responsive logic of machine operation. Machine Intelligence may thus process and assist with complex tasks and large amounts of data. In the architectural discourse, the term has often been associated with implementing information technologies during the whole lifecycle of buildings, from planning to management and operation, by highlighting "smartness" in contemporary urban strategies, like smart-city planning, intelligent buildings, and innovative materials. Today's discourse shifts toward methods of optimization, responsiveness, versatility, and effectiveness in the everyday use of urban structures. Furthermore, the widespread use of artificial intelligence, and machine learning in the architectural field applied with respect to structural and material optimization, reveals further extensive applications and vast territories for architects to explore.

Technologically infused "intelligent" strategies such as machine learning and AI will undoubtedly contribute to developing new types of architecture and architectural thinking. Moreover, there is the promise that such new architecture will be intellectually and spatially more responsive to the natural environment as a whole. Perhaps there will also emerge a new approach to programming for buildings and cities that might challenge the conventional understanding of functionality and instead enable an enhanced multifaceted civic role for architecture.

Ultimately, one hopes that such scientific breakthroughs will inevitably impact the discipline of architecture, raising awareness and providing positive influence with respect to so many vital aspects of architecture. Health and wellbeing, access to knowledge and information, inclusion and equality, and environmental and ecological remediation and repair are a few of the aspects that need to be addressed.

This chapter is dedicated to such notions and probabilities. Presented on the following pages are a series of selected projects that go beyond merely employing automation and new intelligence technologies but

instead investigate the critical impact such information-based technologies will have on urban and architectural thinking and making. Typologies such as housing, learning centers, research & health facilities, and other seemingly prosaic programs are interrogated and revisited. These projects emerge as entirely new forms where architectural "smartness" is embedded into the materials, planning, and aesthetic outcomes. Particular focus is given to educational structures and institutions that safeguard society's collective intellect, with historical, research-oriented, approaches. The shared ambition in these works seeks to create an architecture that intertwines state-of-the-art, information-based technologies with relevant and critical social agendas. The projects seamlessly incorporate cultural trends and novel innovations ranging from communication technologies, mobility concepts, and transformations in modes of production while remaining socially and environmentally aware and relevant. The chapter includes projects that rethink strategies of city planning, cultural and educational buildings, the fate of automation, robotics, and AI, as well as human-machine collaboration within an urban context.

RE_AGGREGATED_CITY
Mass-Customized Spaces

⊗ BRATISLAVA, SLOVAKIA

Located in the old harbor on the Danube River in Bratislava, Slovakia, the project pursues the creation of a city by the aggregation of spatial units, tailored to the needs of their inhabitants and community. The spatial units are built by their users with a system utilizing repurposed robotic arms, creating an interconnectable exterior and mass-customized interior.

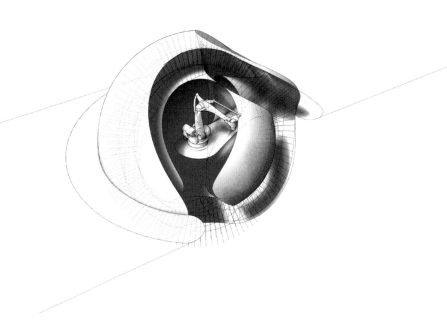

Roman Hajtmanek

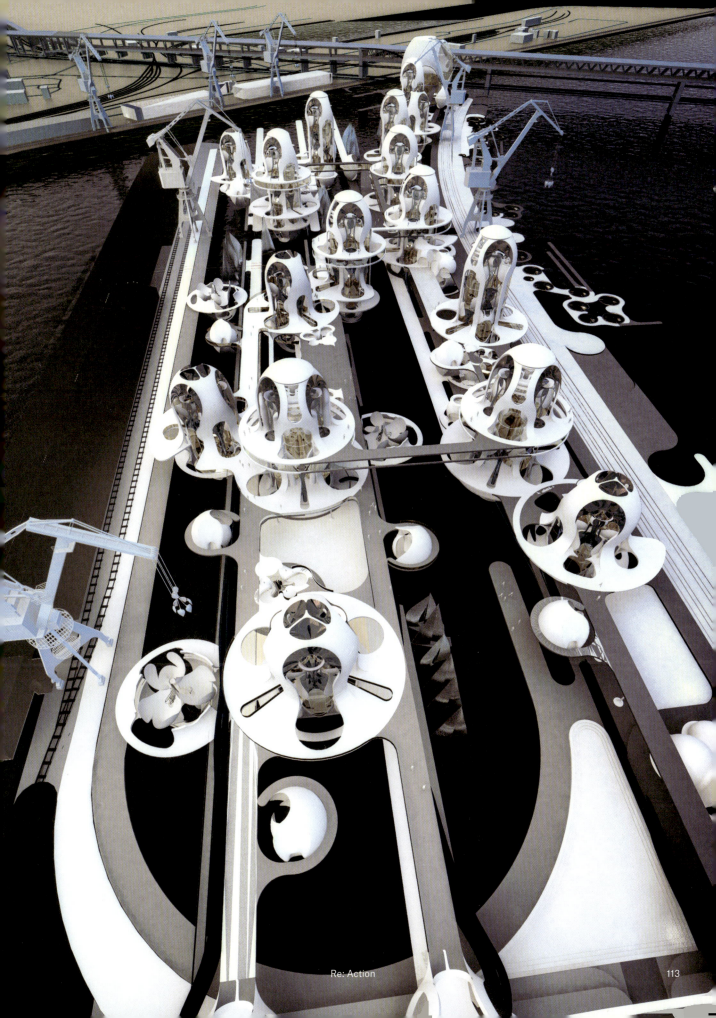

Re: Action

RE_AGGREGATED_CITY

Slovakia is the largest car manufacturer per capita in the world. The project proposes repurposing of outdated robotic arms from the transforming automotive industry for the building sector. In this scenario, robots and humans are becoming one coexisting organism producing new dwellings and living environments. The site of the old harbor is a case study showing how this system could alleviate the local environmental problems of oil pollution from the previous oil refinery and unexpected river floods caused by the climate crisis, as well as providing a sustainable energy source through the utilization of water power. The project also addresses the lack of housing in this region and simultaneously criticizes the simplistic solution to this problem, being the standardization, pre-fabrication, and single-use zoning used in 20th century block housing. Instead of this, it proposes sustainable mass-customized living units adapting to the requirements of the local community.

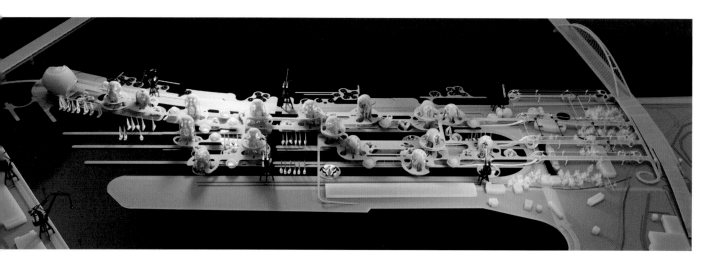

The coexistence of robots and the community is instrumental during, and even after, the building process. In the beginning, the robots are used for building their own infrastructure: cultivating trees, cleaning oil-contaminated soil using tree shoots with contaminants for biomass, building dikes, and building or repairing water turbines for energy production. The inhabitable units for community living are arranged into the larger vertical capsule structures taking a part in the new ecosystem. These structures retain rainwater with water reservoirs placed on the top and utilize the water inside the units. Subsequently, the in-built filtration system at the bottom of the structures filters the water and reuses it in the pollution-cleaning gardens, which further reduces the CO_2 imprint, providing an additional sustainable energy source and creating an environment for recreation. Living in balance with water is further visible in the vertical layering of the project, which creates a space for excess water in the case of floods, but also allows the transport on site by riverboat, interwoven with walkway plateaus, and by the currently existing railway infrastructure and public transport roads on the dike.

The bespoke form of dwellings created by the cooperation of humans and robots is similar to Frederick Kiesler's Endless House, enveloping and aggregating the different activities of its inhabitants. The project is also heavily inspired by Greg Lynn's Embryological House. However, the project proposes not only solitaires of the American dream, but rather mass-customized aggregations similar to Moshe Safdie's Habitat '67.

The units have a tailor-made interior and program, but on the other hand they are also able to be aggregated on their exterior. Connecting different units together, the flexibility and variability of the newly created spaces is increased, in spite of their common formal and geometrical language. The structures are made of thin shells from 3D-printed steel rods and concrete, minimizing the use of materials and maximizing the interior space, aggregating living, working, local production, and recreation. The form of the spatial units is derived from the continuous movements of the printing robotic arm. The movements of the robotic arm are periodical rose curves outlining spheres, tetrahedrons and octahedrons. On the site, four types of units are implemented with distinct uses. The primary units of the project are the cells for living, which are printed directly into vertical capsule-like structures with an embedded robotic infrastructure, water retention and water filtration system. The cells are filled inside these capsule structures according to the needs of the community. The secondary units are cells placed on the site for local community manufacturing, units used in the robotic gardens, cultivating the trees and biomass energy generators.

RE_AGGREGATED_CITY

The new urban quarter is designed to be built by the community itself to improve its environment with the principles of circular economy and ecological sustainability. Opposing the single-use zoning of the 20th century, the project aggregates distinct activities into mass-customized structures with self-generating power abilities for residential, commercial, and light-manufacturing uses.

The collaborative nature of the new development incentivizes the inhabitants to recycle what is no longer usable and share what is not possible to generate individually. Through this, the project ensures a sustainable and balanced co-existence of the community with nature and technology.

A HYBRID FOR ENHANCEMENT
Human Performance Facility

⊗ MOUNT FUJI, JAPAN

A contribution of space and architecture to the revolution of human enhancement in interdependence with our changing environment, near Mount Fuji, Japan.

　Japan, as a country and location, turned out to be a suitable site for the project, based on its long, health-focused culture and its position as a new center of medical technology and research in health and robotics. I choose to place my project next to Mount Fuji, a two-hour drive from Tokyo.

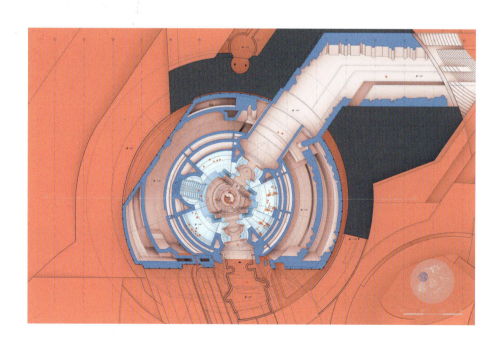

Leonie Eitzenberger

Re: Action

A HYBRID FOR ENHANCEMENT

The site is surrounded by leading robotics companies, military camps, and smart-city projects and is next to an existing private health university.

On the one hand, the project can be seen as an upgrade and expansion of the private health university with the additional idea of making it accessible to international research institutions and teams. On the other hand, it can be considered a contribution to eastern Japan as a new region for research and development, mobility, technology, and healthcare.

Climate change and the increase of natural disasters —and additional consequences such as epidemics and pandemics—will affect the state of human health and wellbeing and these changes will require adaptation, resistance, and immunity.

With the interdependency of our changing environment, we find ourselves in a revolution of enhancement, with its three primary forms: the physical, mental, and artificial/technological. The increase in self-optimization, prevention, monitoring, and health-tracking describes a shift and transformation from care for the sick to healthcare.

"A Hybrid for Enhancement" can be seen as a speculation of architecture as a human-enhancing performance facility to optimize the mental and physical capability of the human form, through the simulation of extreme thermal and climatic conditions and the celebration of science and human-supporting technology. The concept could be rendered as a starting point for special interdisciplinary teams—from sectors like health, the military, and space travel—for people who must perform under extreme conditions in the future.

The architecture is a combination of three main modules that are expressed in a spherical appearance and contribute as a spatial hybrid to human enhancement. The spatial arrangement and program are divided by dynamic and static sequences and singular and plural use of the space.

With the interdependency of our changing environment, we find ourselves in a revolution of enhancement, with its three primary forms: the physical, mental, and artificial/technological. The increase in self-optimization, prevention, monitoring, and healthtracking describes a shift and transformation from care for the sick to healthcare.

A HYBRID FOR ENHANCEMENT

The composition is arranged next to the existing university. The continuity of the circulation creates connectivity between the three main modules, integrates the university, and creates a public square at the intersection point. Connectivity is also the basis for incisions in the building for access, natural light, and the design of facade elements. The three modules are divided into the following:

The simulation of microclimates aims to optimize the adaptation in artificially simulated, extreme climatic conditions.

As a starting point, the inner-space conditions will focus on hot/cold, high humidity, and less oxygen.

A central pool for anti-gravity exercise is surrounded by microclimate capsules with individual and plural-use possibilities.

The vertical arrangement of the four main categories of the climate condition, and the use of concrete panels that include solar fluid, gives the possibility to use solar heat as the main supplier and use the return flow of the heaters for cooling. Summarizing the process, the fluid heated by the sun is compressed in the compressor and becomes even hotter. After that, it starts to expand and cool and, over the process, becomes warm again and will be modified to cool.

The second module, the self-factory, can be seen as a stage for research and science. It celebrates the new interpretation of an anatomical theater and the kinematics of technology, and offers space for research in medical and pharmaceutical/biotechnological approaches. The main space can be seen as a stage for science and opens up a new interaction between human-enhancing technology and humans.

The testing facility of human-supporting technology is for testing enhancing prosthetics and exoskeletons under radiation, water, and pressure, for example.

The shells of the three modules will consist of pre-fabricated concrete elements with an oscillating swinging shell as a foundation, connected with earthquake-absorbing dampers in a form of coupled tension members and damping springs.

The project can be seen as architecture that is not just shelter, but more a preparation for seemingly uninhabitable extreme climatic conditions. It aims to serve as an architectural apparatus and spatial facilitator for human enhancement.

DELIRIOUS CAMPUS
Neo-Metabolist Approach
for Medical Startup Infrastructure

⊗ GENEVA, SWITZERLAND

"The concept of a rebirth of metabolism in architecture, which envisions a fundamentally new approach for medical startup infrastructure."

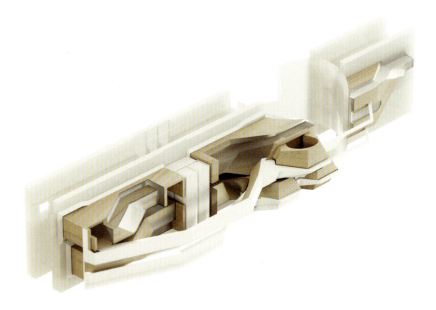

Dennis Karandiuk

124 Intelligent_Architecture

DELIRIOUS CAMPUS

Switzerland has an extraordinary variety of landscapes, ranging from the Central Plateau to the high peaks of the Alps.[1] Its inhabitants have a wide history of interacting with the surrounding nature in an extremely respectful way. Incorporating urban infrastructure into different topographic conditions with outstanding accuracy, the Swiss have managed to create locations that resemble the unique appearance of a "jumble of jigsaw pieces." That's why one of the anchor points of the project was to encapsulate traditional Swiss urban DNA into the design proposal. At the same time, it was important to reinforce the project with contemporary vision, future-oriented technologies, and profound design, which will respond to all upcoming challenges of the med-tech industry, which is undergoing rapid growth.

The design proposal is a new vision of architectural ideas investigated by the Metabolism movement in the '60s. Nowadays, with the use of technologies and AI, we are able to collect and analyze data from the everyday behavior of campus users. We are able to create responsive infrastructure by building a research campus that incorporates a wide range of kinetic and modular elements that respond and interact with collected data. Modularity not only improves the performance of a campus, it also lowers expenses for maintenance of the premises.
The vertical primary structure for module stacking provides an opportunity to optimize the building footprint and prevent the appearance of abandoned infrastructure in the future. All the modules can be relocated and repurposed according to needs. From a long-term perspective, all this decreases energy consumption for building maintenance as well as lowers the carbon footprint for initial construction and demolition at the end of a building's lifespan.

The project goals are to achieve an increase in efficiency in the performance of medical startups on both the micro and macro levels. To achieve this, the design proposal includes an innovative approach of utilizing modular architecture that turns static infrastructure into a dynamic "living organism" that lives and evolves along with the user activity inside it. Architectural strategy itself accompanies the latest med-tech startup management schemes. By programming clusters with all the necessary equipment for research and development, this design proposal provides the ability to efficiently restructure premises clusters to respond to the growth and shrinking of particular research teams. Moreover, such an approach helps to increase cross-team collaboration. Teams with high synergetic potential can be relocated to be at a close distance from each other to increase their efficiency in collaboration.

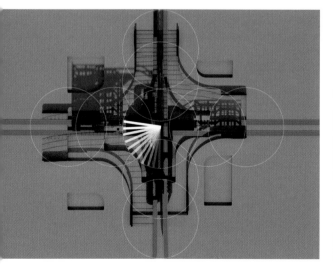
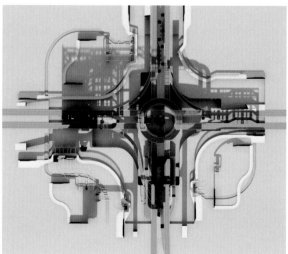

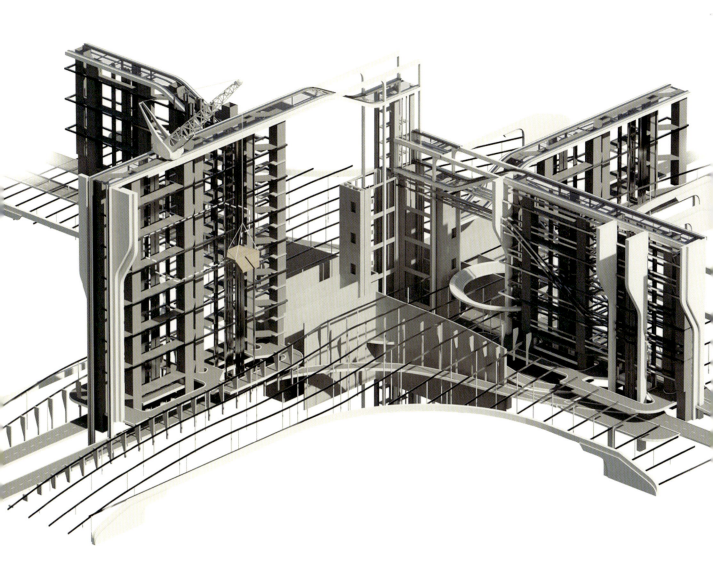

1   "Urban and Spatial Development," The Federal Department of Foreign Affairs Switzerland, February 19, 2021, www.eda.admin.ch/aboutswitzerland/en/home/umwelt/geografie/staedtebau-und-raumentwicklung.html.

DELIRIOUS CAMPUS

Metabolic approach not only helps to create efficient infrastructure for the initial purpose, but also has great potential for sustainable urban growth. On a macro scale, it represents a high level of adaptability, which means that all clusters can be repurposed at the end of their life cycle for the new needs of local society. Additionally, the primary construction material for modules is locally produced cross-laminated timber, which is a fully renewable resource. As a result, the architectural concept, along with the choice of material, helps decrease the carbon footprint of production, transportation, and maintenance—as well as energy consumption over the full lifecycle of a building—ensuring a sustainable urban future.

One of the anchor points of the project was to encapsulate traditional Swiss urban DNA into the design proposal. At the same time, it was important to reinforce the project with contemporary vision, future-oriented technologies, and profound design, which will respond to all upcoming challenges of the med-tech industry, which is undergoing rapid growth.

URBAN LEARNING HUB
The Academic Campus of Tomorrow

⊗ SAN JOSE, USA

Monika Kalinowska

130　　　　　　　　　　　Intelligent_Architecture

Re: Action

UNIVERSITY 4.0
Kinetic Campus

⊗ MOSCOW, RUSSIA

Anna Tuzova

134   Intelligent_Architecture

Re: Action

UNIVERSITY 4.0

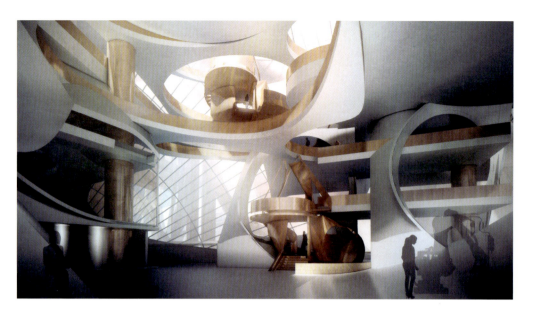

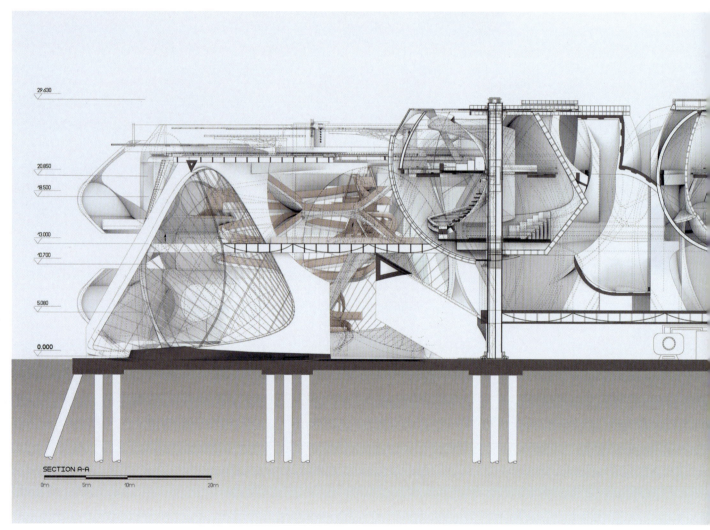

SECTION A-A
0m   5m   10m   20m

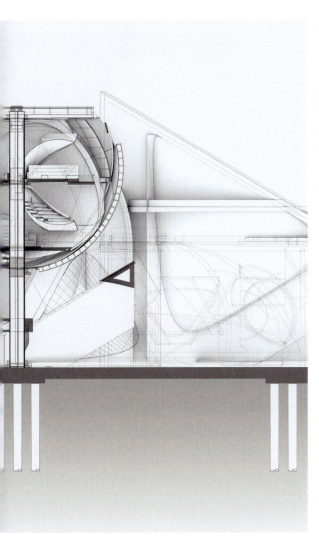

URBAN REDEMPTION
A Plug-in Urban Redemption
in the Paradigm of New Technology

⊗ SAN FRANCISCO BAY, USA

Dennis Karandiuk

138 Intelligent_Architecture

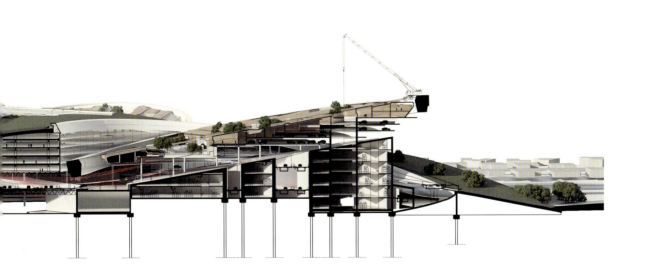

Re: Action

URBAN REDEMPTION

THE EUTOPIAN FACTORY
An Alternative to the Industrial Exploitation

⊗ TALVIVAARA SOTKAMO, FINLAND

Jan Kovaříček

THE EUTOPIAN FACTORY

Using shell analysis to produce streamlines that inform the main directionality of the CLT

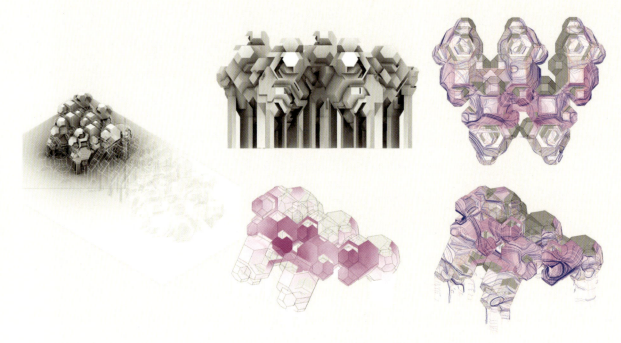

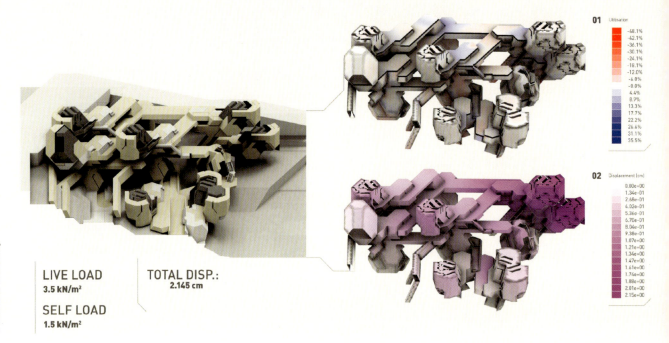

Structural feasibility

LIVE LOAD
3.5 kN/m²

SELF LOAD
1.5 kN/m²

TOTAL DISP.:
2.145 cm

144   Intelligent_Architecture

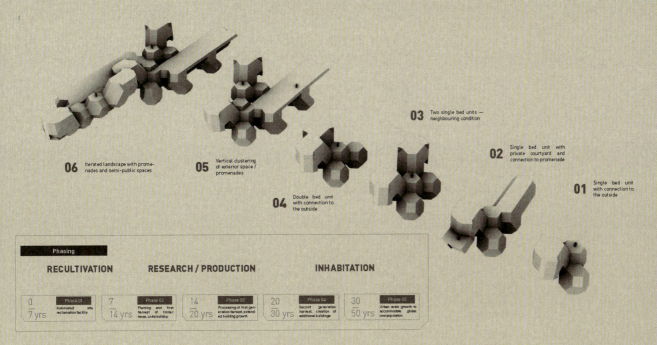

06 Iterated landscape with promenades and semi-public spaces
05 Vertical clustering of exterior space / promenades
04 Double bed unit with connection to the outside
03 Two single bed units — neighbouring condition
02 Single bed unit with private courtyard and connection to promenade
01 Single bed unit with connection to the outside

Phasing

| RECULTIVATION | RESEARCH / PRODUCTION | INHABITATION |

0 / 7 yrs — Phase 01 — Automated site reclamation facility
7 / 14 yrs — Phase 02 — Planting and first harvest of timber trees, units buildup
14 / 20 yrs — Phase 03 — Processing of first generation harvest, extended building growth
20 / 30 yrs — Phase 04 — Second generation harvest, creation of additional buildings
30 / 50 yrs — Phase 05 — Urban scale growth to accommodate global overpopulation

01 Octahedron as a boundary guide for spatial element
02 Archetype — hybrid column / plateau inscribed in a boundary guide

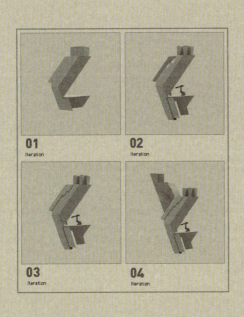

01 Iteration
02 Iteration
03 Iteration
04 Iteration

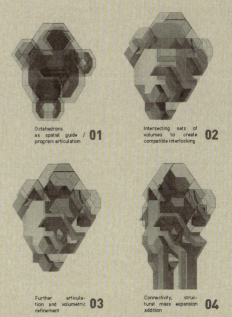

01 Octahedrons as spatial guide / program articulation
02 Intersecting sets of volumes to create compatible interlocking
03 Further articulation and volumetric refinement
04 Connectivity, structural mass expansion addition

Catalogue

Geometry Concept / Combining the logic of interlocking to non-uniform elements

Re: Action 145

SONIC BLUR
An Audiovisual VR Exhibition and Physical Installation Staging Selected Work of the Institute of Architecture

Studio Hani Rashid's curatorial contribution for the Angewandte Festival 2021 celebrates human interconnectivity and communication through the interplay between virtual collaboration environments and in situ installations, showcasing the diversity of the institute's annual student works.

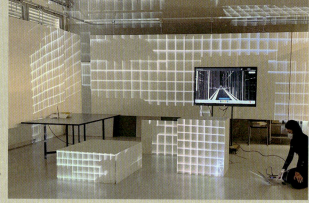

STUDIO HANI RASHID
Exhibition Design: Sarah Agill, Raffael Stegfellner

"Sonic Blur" consists of a continuous striated landscape that seamlessly spans from a virtual exhibition platform easily accessible from any web browser, where visitors can communicate and interact while meandering among the works on display, to its physical counterpart in the main exhibition space at the Institute of Architecture.

The virtual show, developed by the studio's students Sarah Agill and Raffael Stegfellner, forms a cluster of immersive structured landscapes. As the participants move through the digital halls, the overlapping of different traces intuitively leads them further into the mist of space. The tubular aggregation offers cues of the familiar but fuses them with plays on scale and weightlessness.

Along the pathways, a carefully curated sonic trail accompanies the viewer through space, framing a synaesthetic composition where sound becomes palpable while the visual stays shifting as part of a continuously synchronized choreography. The distribution of the sonic and visual queues highlight ambiguous hints of action in the distance. As the virtual experience becomes an exploration of sensory stimulation in the sphere of complete immateriality, the physical exhibition at the institute hosts the physical models and works of the departments and broadcasts the virtual show on screens, offering a seamless experience between the digital and the physical environment.

Invocation for Hope by Superflux (© Stefan Lux)

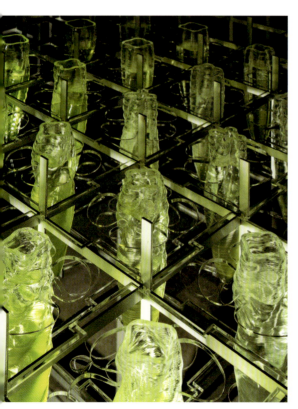
BITBIOBOT by ecoLogicStudio (© Marco Cappelletti)

148 Panel Talk: Corrective Methodologies and Architectural Futures

Panel Talk

Corrective Methodologies and Architectural Futures

Anab Jain
Greg Lynn
Timothy Morton
Claudia Pasquero
Hani Rashid

Panel Talk:
Corrective Methodologies and Architectural Futures

PARTICIPANTS
Anab Jain, Greg Lynn, Timothy Morton, Claudia Pasquero, Hani Rashid

DATE
April 25, 2022

Hani Rashid It is a pleasure to have some extraordinarily inspired and remarkable panelists on this Zoom panel today. A group that we have managed to bring together to speak on specific subjects and the provocations that we've placed under the rubric "Corrected Methodologies and Architectural Futures." The panel will take a deep dive into the future of our discipline.

Architectural theory and practice have been, in recent years, increasingly in a state of extreme turbulence and uncertain flux, driven predominantly by critical environmental issues, particularly those of resilience and environmental sustainability, significantly as these phenomena impact the future of our cities and architecture. The sad realities of the many humanitarian crises and emergencies we are witnessing in many locations across the globe are very much the result of a confluence of environmental, economic, migratory, sanitary, and political vectors. These factors increasingly impact all aspects of humanity and civic life across the planet.

Today, radical shifts in our discipline, and related practices in particular, necessitate the need to confront and engage many crucial issues to combat an all too powerful and prevailing sense of uncertainty and unpredictability for the future of humankind. There is now an indisputable necessity for explicit strategies of what I'd call a need for an architecture of repair and reconciliation. Radical architectural and engineering visions are today not an option but rather an absolute necessity.

Vital, robust, and perhaps even far-fetched architectural and urban visionary concepts and designs must be produced, especially in architecture schools. There is a dire need for works and ideas centered on being effective as an enduring defense of humankind's basic needs and welfare for the near future. Moreover, [works and ideas] with a mandate to be corrective measures for the health and welfare of the planet and our ecosystems. So, on that premise, today we will hear from four remarkable innovators and profound thinkers on these subjects—each of their approaches and visions for the future of our cities and societies are quite illuminating.

The first of our four speakers is Claudia Pasquero. Claudia is an architect, curator, author, and educator. Her work and research operates at the intersection between biology, computation, and design. Claudia is co-founder (with Marco Poletto) and director of the London-based studio ecoLogicStudio that, since its founding in 2005, has built a unique portfolio of biophilic sculptures, living architectures, and what they call "blue-green master plans." And, in 2012, they published *Systemic Architecture: Operating Manual for the Self-Organizing City*.

Claudia has a distinguished academic career. She is Professor of Landscape Architecture at Innsbruck University, where she also heads the Institute of Urban Design and is founder of the Synthetic Landscape Lab. She is also an associate professor at The Bartlett School of Architecture, where she directs the Urban Morphogenesis Lab. Her work has been published and exhibited internationally at the Frac Centre in Orléans (France), the Venice Biennale, ZKM Karlsruhe, Milan Expo 2015, and EXPO Astana 2017. In 2018, ecoLogicStudio launched Photo.Synthetica, an innovative venture into a partnership with the Urban Morphogenesis Lab at The Bartlett in London and the Synthetic Landscapes Lab at Innsbruck University. Together they have developed scalable nature-based design solutions, nature-based solutions to the imminent impact of climate

change and our contemporary quest for carbon neutrality. Their current and recent exhibitions showcase ecoLogicStudio's work on the future of green urban planning, combining AI and extensive data analysis where they understand the true nature of contemporary cities as a complex dynamical system and built environment.
Human systems regularly interact with green spaces where the human system and green spaces interact. Cities are evolving into super-intelligent organisms involving human and non-human citizens. Without further ado, I turn the Zoom stage over to Claudia.

Claudia Pasquero

Thank you. At ecoLogicStudio we design the living. We are often told that we are in a time of climate change, but change is an inherent quality of the planet we inhabit. Architecture, intended as an interface between humans and environment, between the human and the non-human, could possibly enable a different relationship to change. Rather than stopping change, we could start to establish positive dynamics of change. We can start by referring to biological models whose aesthetic constitute a meta-language of patterns of change that reveal fundamental aspects of their ecological intelligence. To articulate these thoughts through design examples, I would like to illustrate today the work of the Photo.Synthetica venture.

The Photo.Synthetica venture was established by ecoLogicStudio London (co-founded with Marco Poletto in 2005), in conjunction with the main academic partners, Innsbruck University and The Bartlett, UCL. The consortium has ever since developed test beds and pilot projects globally.

The focus has been on designing the Urbansphere, the growing network of infrastructures of matter, information and energy, fueling the metabolism of contemporary cities. We have been proposing a model to move from the current metabolically linear city, which we inherited from modernity, to a metabolically circular one. The latter would be structured through multiple interactive networks of collective intelligence, where each unit, down in scale to the single dwelling, becomes a nucleus of re-metabolization of waste and production of resources.

At Photo.Synthetica we ask ourselves: can we convert what cities expel as waste or pollution into healthy super-food and sustainable materials for a growing urban population? The core biological engine of our photosynthetic architectures is, more specifically, microalgae, one of the oldest organisms on Earth. Microalgae populate the water bodies of the whole planet. Their proliferation is also an unwanted consequence of global warming, it is called "algae blooming." Algae bloom as they are able to feed on the many byproducts of our society, such as for example the wasteful emissions of the farming industry that end up in the oceans. And in doing so, unexpectedly, algae already contribute to the emergence of circular ecologies in the Urbansphere. Today, 50% of the world's CO_2 is absorbed and stored in oceans by powerful photosynthetic microalgae. Photo.Synthetica, as an architectural venture, combines design innovation and microbiology to create artificial habitats to grow algae collectively in the urban realm. This enables us to tap into some of the unique photosynthetic characteristics of microalgae to turn the polluted, for us, urban atmosphere into a fertile ground for re-metabolization. In other words, we can turn pollutants into nutrients and literally mine the urban atmosphere for resources.

Powered by the sun, algae captures and stores CO_2 molecules and air pollutants into biomass, enabling new circular economies of food and biomaterials. If we move from the linear city to a different diagram of re-metabolization, then CO_2 and NO_2, PM2.5, PM10, molecules and particles that we call "pollutants" because they affect our health negatively, these all become food for other organisms, thus becoming an input into a new line of synthesis. Data, biomass and oxygen are the output that feed multiple spatial and material processes as well as the economy of the food, pharmaceutical and biomaterial industries among others.

[Video]

We are now so many and our impact on the biosphere is so large and so vast that biological systems cannot adapt fast enough. Therefore, we design human gardens as a form of interface between multiple forms of intelligence, human as well as non-human, and between the built environment and the natural one[.]

Re: Action

CP   H.O.R.T.U.S. XL Astaxanthin.g is a large-scale, high-resolution 3D-printed bio-digital sculpture commissioned by the Centre Pompidou in Paris in 2019 for the exhibition "La Fabrique du vivant." It's 3D-printed in algae-based bioplastic and live microalgae colonies on bio-gel medium are inoculated accordingly to a bio-pixels' matrix. It's a sculpture but at the same time it's a fragment of architecture, informed by a larger architectural concept called "Photo.Synthetica tower." This large urban organism enables the new practice of cyber-gardening as an open relationship between humans and the urban environment.

In this image we see exhibited in Tokyo at the Mori gallery what this larger assemblage could look like. Its façade populated not only with microalgae reactors but also larger and more complex vertical landscape ecologies, becoming a stopover for migratory birds and allowing the emergence of ecosystemic experimentation right in the dense city center. We have tested the actualization of this concept at multiple scales and forms. The BIO.tech Hut, for instance, was presented at EXPO Astana 2017 as a prototype dwelling and remains today as a permanent photosynthetic architecture within the museum of future energy.

It's composed of a science lab where we can learn about the property of microalgae, an art experience environment where the user is encouraged to interact with the morphology, aesthetic, and spatial articulation of architectural photosynthesis, as well as the craft and production garden where every two weeks the biomass from the multiple species of the microalgae is harvested. The BIO.tech Hut is able to photosynthesize an amount of CO_2 similar to a small urban forest, as well as to produce proteins that are equivalent to the one that will be produced by breeding approximately eight cows. Recently we've further investigated these aspects in the public realm, through the Air Bubble playground for instance. This is a two-year long research project in partnership with GSK pharmaceutical and their respiratory health brand Otrivin. We will now see a very short video, developed in collaboration with Saatchi & Saatchi in London, to communicate the project and the issues around the respiratory health of children in contemporary cities.

[Video]   *I feel stacked in the middle. Do I send them out to play in pollution or keep them locked up inside? It's a major problem. Pollution levels are far worse at child's height. They are more sensitive to the detrimental effects of air pollution.*

We all grew up going outside and not having to worry about things. I never thought I'd have to protect my kids from the one thing that keeps them alive. As a mom, it breaks my heart. I just want to play. [...]

Microalgae are incredible organisms and with our technology we can use them to clean our cities' air. We have gone to one of Europe's most polluted areas and built the world's first air-purifying biotechnological playground. The uniqueness of this concept relies on the relationship between the architecture and the kids. The more children play, the more the algae absorbs pollutants and clean oxygen is released. This algae is what's taking the bad stuff out of the air. [...]

The air here is amazing. The key aspect of this project is to create awareness that it is indeed possible to clean the air we breathe. This can't be the only way to help them breathe better. We need to do more.

re-metabolization

CP   One of the key aspects of this project was how to discuss the question of re-metabolization of air pollution in the urban atmosphere. And in this case, I use "re-metabolization" rather than "cleaning" on purpose because algae effectively re-metabolizes elements that are dangerous for us and create nutritious aliments that we can consume, rather than simply cleaning the city for us which implies moving the residue somewhere else out of sight.

When I was talking to different stakeholders about the project, I realized that many were looking at the playground with a reductionist perspective that considers architecture a mere scaffolding onto which we could attach our innovative nature-based technology. I explained that architecture can do much more. The challenge was to discuss how the overall morphology or form and the design of the playground was a critical ingredient in the trans-scalar interaction with the surrounding environment and the kids.

In directing the air flow as well as instigating kids' playfulness for instance. It is the architecture after all that contributes to the activation of the microalgae and their transformative action on the air surrounding the playground.

In this case study, we also had a set of sensors embedded in the playground and we measured air pollution concentrations inside and outside the playground as well as in other neighborhoods in Warsaw. Inside the playground we recorded reductions of up to 79% of PM2.5 and PM10, NO_2 and CO_2 concentrations compared to immediate surroundings. These are some of the diagrams that show the air quality index and its fluctuations in time.

Recently we have carried forward this project on a second, deployable version of Air Bubble, demonstrating our vision for an architecture of carbon neutrality. This was unveiled at COP26 in Glasgow in November 2021 and later traveled to Saudi Arabia for the first Art Biennale. It is a pneumatic structure, 99% made up of microalgae, air, and water. It is wrapped by a three-dimensional membrane of TPU of only 0.5 mm of thickness. The sounds, odors, light reflections and soft floating floor and walls all have transformative action, contributing to the perception of architecture as a living non-human being. Again, we have played here with a certain sense of enhanced integration of parts into an emergent architectural whole capable of independent behavior. The 200-square-meter architecture is 6m tall and only weighs eighty kilos when empty, which makes it easily deployable. Of course, we inoculate a local species of microalgae in every location, Riyadh being very different from Glasgow.

In the project we presented at the last Venice architecture Biennale in 2021, titled "Bit.Bio.Bot," we focused on a more domestic dimension, articulating the co-existence with non-human living species within the dwelling in what can be defined as a personal microbiological garden. Here the element of pleasure finds center stage and is embodied into 36 3D printed crystals. This glassware collection is the result of a collaboration with Swarovski and offers a new spectacle of feeding ourselves with algae based proteic concoctions.

This project has been spinning off recently into a commercial venture for a home photobioreactor, the BioBombola. Another spinoff is venturing into commercial office environments. We have been collaborating with Nestle to retrofit their factory into a bio-building able to grow on its walls raw ingredients feeding into their production line. The first prototype is now built in the Nestle headquarters in Lisbon.

In conclusion from these projects, we have learned that when architecture becomes capable of synthesizing resources, it is no longer a container of programs or functions, like in the modern machine for living, and becomes a dynamic process of production, a living machine. This, of course, has great repercussions at the urban scale too. Current centralized infrastructures, such as the energy or waste water networks, could become distributed and collective, with each urban dwelling becoming a center for re-metabolization and production as well as consumption and exchange. It is a new kind of collective intelligence that emerges for a vision of a city as a cognitive being.

We visualized this scenario for the future of Tallinn in a project called Anthropocene Island developed by ecoLogicStudio for the Tallinn Architecture Biennale 2017 that I curated. Another vision for a cognitive city has been on show at the Centre Pompidou in 2021 and is now part of its permanent collection. It's called the GAN-Physarum, and features the biological intelligence of a slime mold, physarum polycephalum, deployed to train a GAN machine learning algorithm to envision a future green/blue Paris. Here are some frames from the exhibition.

This is a zoom-in, for instance, of the large biological simulation we run over Paris, captured in a video sequence. The animation shows the transformation of Paris in time and from a scale of ten kilometers square down to one hundred meters, centered on the building of the Centre Pompidou.

[V] [00:24:55–00:25:50]

CP   It feels like the right kind of frame to end this presentation, visualizing the world's best example of a dynamic architectural machine being re-metabolized into a wet, soft, living tissue of photosynthetic surfaces and fluid connective vessels. Thank you.

HR Claudia, thank you. That was a brilliant presentation. I wanted to ask you a couple of things. As I was watching, I thought,

"In the history of our discipline it's difficult to point to a specific moment, other than post-WWII, where architects obsessively and effectively exposed so much disarray and chaos."

Furthermore, by doing so, reality and truth are put forth through architecture as something people should be provoked to react to and not passively endure. Therefore, what I find fascinating about the work is the implicit idea that the discourse is centered on exposure of cause and effect and thereby made explicit and tangible. I think that what is interesting about that approach is that it puts us in a position to comprehend the gravity of the present situation. The absolute necessity to clean the air we collectively breathe or create food and sustenance from waste is ultimately an architecture centered on repair.

I wonder if you could perhaps speak a little further on the nature of your preoccupation with these all-essential aspects of betterment and repair. I appreciate that you are creating a new and exciting aesthetic condition, making the work visually appealing and seductive. Doing so puts us intellectually in a position to rethink and comprehend many critical issues at a visceral level. I believe what is so vivid in your work is essentially what science and architecture have always had in common, where technology has played the protagonist, perhaps to a fault, making one believe that everything needs to be efficient, clean, and smooth. Our air conditioning comes out magically from clean, white, shrink-wrapped machines and the like.

For example, I think of the likes of certain 20th-century art luminaries such as Joseph Beuys or George Maciunas and his Fluxus group. The art world, especially in the 20th century, had invested much in unraveling and exposing the underbelly of the hollow promises of a technologically focused future—a world view that we are increasingly subscribing to and relentlessly pummeling towards. So, I think that you, as an architect, are on a fascinating trajectory in light of confronting the future and the future of technology as it pertains to our discipline. I wonder if you wanted to talk a little bit about these aspects because, above all I just mentioned, the work is stunning. It is interesting that, along with all the intelligence and logic, at the end of the day, the work is simply beautiful.

CP Yes, in a way I often speculate on the fact that when the name "architecture" came about in the Renaissance in Florence the relationship between what we call the Urbansphere and the living Biosphere was inverted. There was a social, political and perhaps ecological reason for architecture to be a fortress, framed through the perspective view. Now this relationship has totally changed. Architecture as a framing interface should really become an intensifier of communication, thus exposing its infrastructure, the dynamic flows that underpin its interaction with the living Biosphere. You said this correctly, it is art that exposes it. Or architecture's artistic dimension. I think it's great that it has been exposed, but now it's time to reconstruct it. So, how do we reconstruct what it has been exposed to? In this sense, I think that the aesthetic of architecture, as a meta-language, has a role to play, even a political role, in defining new ecologies of technology. We have scientific development that too often cannot be embedded, it cannot be collectively appropriated unless the end user develops a daily practice on interaction with it. And this appropriation is enabled by aesthetic languages. This is critical in enabling transformative practices to emerge locally and then connect globally, with a radical impact on the planet and the living Biosphere.

That's where I think the role of aesthetics becomes critical. That's why I often start a project from the prototypical component, enabling an immediate intimate interaction, a meaningful experience that can be communicated and proliferated across scales thus achieving significant impact in the medium and long terms.

HR   I was thinking about Lars Spuybroek when I saw your Frac Centre involvement in Orléans on your resume. I remember having an exhibition alongside Lars at the Frac and I recall that he exhibited a new concept for mass housing that he explored well before the advent of 3D printing. His idea at the time was centered on designing and building a large housing complex where people would be given the opportunity and means to reconfigure their architecture. This was possible according to various numeric systems and dynamics that Lars dreamed up, including rudimentary milling and manufacturing technologies. For example, families fluctuating in size, be that growth or diminishing in size, would be part of the data feed around which the architecture dynamics would shift the shape and outcome of the design. His notion of constantly reconfiguring architecture was remarkably prescient, especially considering the technologies we now have at our disposal.

Furthermore, as I watched your presentation, I started thinking that the philosophy or mindset of a person living in a home and watching the very things they consume transform from waste to nutrition is quite powerful. This leads one to think about the prospects of being able to reconfigure one's psychological space alongside the formal spatiality one dwells in. If we think of the history and presence of tract housing and suburban planning, especially in America, the kind of sprawl that all these houses create, the rampant burning of fossil fuels, and the waste of materials—it would be a compelling future when we all become aware of these aspects and can rethink a cradle-to-grave logic and philosophy. So, are you interested in mass housing because it would be amazing to think about what that would be like from your studio?

CP   Yes. My main interest has always been, a little bit in a Machiavellian way, infrastructure, because I think it has not been considered enough in the architectural realm. In fact, the Pompidou somehow is a project that is very dear to me because it emerged from this idea of an endlessly reconfigurable building that is appropriated by the people that use it, inhabit it and live or work in it. It blurred typological boundaries and patterns of use, at least theoretically.

The relationship between collective infrastructure and mass housing then becomes very relevant. In my work I explored this relationship in the Anthropocene Island and the Photo.Synthetica tower projects, favoring high-density solutions. In the first case as an extension of a synthetic infrastructural landscape that intensifies its metabolism and becomes inhabitable. In the latter as a vertical cluster of metabolic units.

A new direction is envisioned by the Bit.Bio.Bot. village as imagined in the Venice lagoon; a distinctively horizontal system that attempts to re-interpret the ubiquitous typology of the industrial big shed into an inhabited productive cluster.

But as I said we often put the accent on the infrastructural side of the coin because we think the interactions with flows of matter and energy are often not considered as design generators. We are advocating a shift from designing morphologies to designing morphogenetic processes. Of course, without forgetting that morphology is perhaps the most tangible instance of morphogenesis.

HR   I think the powerful thing is that your work can be read scientifically and as proof-of-concept and poetically as a dream-like spatiality. I think there is something extraordinary in that overlap, which could lead the way to a more sustainable future for our discipline because I believe humankind and the planet require expertise that, once realigned, we as architects can bring forward and provide. I think what you showed us is right on the mark. Thank you very much.

We will continue. Now I would like to introduce the second speaker, Timothy Morton.

I am super honored to have them join us today on this panel. Timothy is a philosopher and a literary theorist who has collaborated with a diverse group of individuals ranging from Björk, Jennifer Walshe, Jeff Bridges, Sabrina Scott, and Pharrell Williams. Timothy has taught at the University of Colorado Boulder, NYU, and UC Davis. Since 2012, they have been a professor at Rice University.

Timothy's work has been translated into ten languages and includes authoring over fifteen books and two hundred essays on philosophy, ecology, literature, music, art, architecture, design, and food. Timothy's books have focused on ecology critique, beginning with *Ecology without Nature* in 2007 and *The Ecological Thought* in 2012, and have argued for the necessity of entirely rejecting our current concept of nature instead of adopting a radical new approach. Subsequent writings expand on this with concepts such as mesh, dark ecology, and hyperobjects. They argue that our ecological catastrophe has occurred already, that all beings relate to each other in a totalizing open system and that humans need to radically rethink how they conceive of and relate to non-human animals of nature as a whole.

Among Timothy's many collaborations, they co-wrote and appeared in *Living in the Future's Past*, a 2018 film with Jeff Bridges about global warming that aims to provide fresh insights into our subconscious motivations and their unintended consequences and show us how no one can predict how significant changes might emerge from the spontaneous actions of the many, how energy takes many forms and moves through and animates everything, and how we come to understand our genuine connection to all that there is. By preparing for something entirely different, we need to redefine our expectations not as to what we will lose but what we might gain. So, Timothy, the Zoom floor is yours.

Timothy Morton   Thank you for that very kind introduction. How much time do I have left?

 HR As much as you would like.

TM Okay. I think on the whole, that isn't even hard, as Claudia has so beautifully shown.
This takes a slight shift in perspective, really. I'm going around now trying to tell people what if it was too easy to become more ecologically attuned to people, making things that would be of benefit to humans and non-humans alike. And what if that was actually too easy, so that people like me make it sound really complicated because we think we need to get paid—thank you for almost laughing—by intimidating people into feeling stupid.

There is a kind of stupid, that I'm actually…a symptom of me is a kind of stupidity, which is a kind of intellectual stupidity. I've got thousands of footnotes; why I should retain these ideas and not those ideas? It's actually more of a kind of diamond-hard stupidity than your average stupidity. I'm just saying this word, I'm getting you ready because I'm going to be talking about—forgive me—idiots, so that you don't have to. I think it was actually beautiful, thank you for smiling.

Basically, first of all, I did this dialogue with Slavoj Žižek a couple of weeks ago. We basically just shouted at each other in agreement for about two hours. It was transcribed and it's coming out in a real review, part of it, in a few weeks' time, Jack Self's *Real Review*. At the end, he said…and I may not be able to imitate his accent properly …he basically said, "With people I don't really like, I tell them how wonderful it was and what a great dialogue we had and how amazing and fantastic ideas we had. But for you I reserve my highest compliment. You are not a complete idiot." Now I want on the back of all of my books: "'Timothy Morton is not a complete,' with italics, *'complete idiot'* — Slavoj Žižek."

Thirteen languages—no one told me there's a Turkish *Hyperobjects*. People don't tell me these things and I don't really care about them or pay them much attention. So suddenly, I found out four years ago—well, maybe two years ago—that a Turkish translation of *Hyperobjects* was published. So, I think *Dark Ecology, Humankind*, and *Hyperobjects*, you can get in Turkish, yay.

Synthetic landscapes. We're both doing it. It was David Ruy, he sort of contacted me and said, "Would you like to do this thing?" Who knows, maybe it's a synchronous thing that happened. But basically, we're just trying to reimagine what quote-unquote "landscape" brackets [A] architecture could be. One of the reasons why is to have a propositional persuasive effect on people. Again, I'm going to talk about idiots: how do you convince your brain to the ecological? You can have all these ideas; clearly, we're not

156 Panel Talk: Corrective Methodologies and Architectural Futures

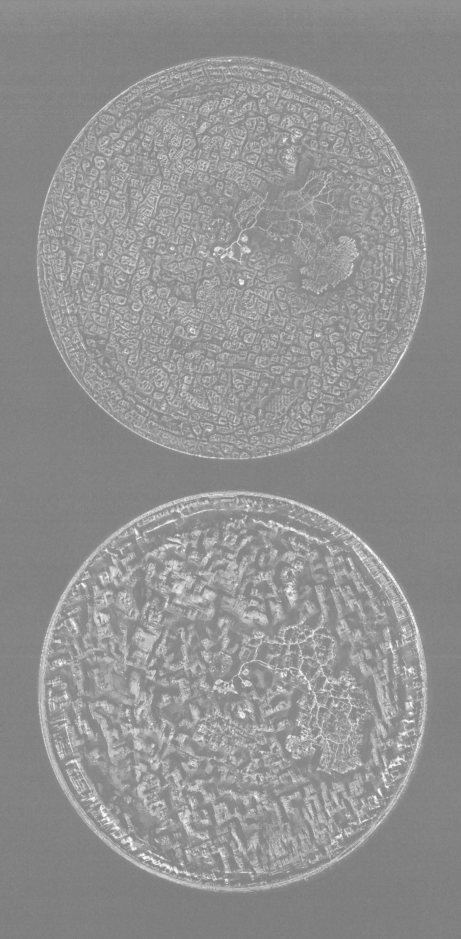

GAN-Physarum: la dérive numérique, video frames from GAN-Physarum evolution in Paris (scale of the city map, 3×3 km) (© ecoLogicStudio)

GAN-Physarum: la dérive numérique, video frames from GAN-Physarum evolution in Paris, Centre Pompidou neighborhood Beaubourg area (scale of the city map, 1×1 km) (© ecoLogicStudio)

acting on them well enough. Why? In part, it's because we need everybody on our side for this, just like with COVID, which I got last week by the way, because my son was in a restaurant and forced to wear no mask with no one with a mask. All the staff not wearing a mask either. It was an old conservative restaurant; you can imagine some anti-vax people were there. So, I got COVID. The virus doesn't care if you're smart or an idiot. But also, a building doesn't care so much how smart you are. It forces you to inhabit the world in a certain way. This is kind of what we're talking about here. We're talking about how we need to work with people's brain. I'm very much on the side of the brain these days rather than the mind. Actually, it reminds me of a joke, another joke that Slavoj tells about a chicken. You know this one, right? There's a guy. He's paranoid he's being persecuted by a giant chicken. So, he goes to a sanatorium. He spends a few weeks there. He's cured of his paranoia. A few weeks later, he comes back to the sanatorium crying, "Why are the sheep terrified? Oh my God, it's the chicken!" Ah, you know, and the head psychiatrist is like, "But you know, there's no chicken" and he's like, "Yeah, but try telling that to the chicken."

Now, the brain is basically a kind of chicken, isn't it? And it's kind of sitting in this egg called your skull. And it's how to talk to the chicken, right? I spend most of my life trying to invent sentences that will talk also to the chicken. It's my great honor to help people doing architecture. I have no idea about the load-bearing properties of materials but I have some sense of how to talk to the chicken and we need to talk to the chicken. My sense of what that is...to get the chicken to feel more like a scientist actually. So, I was struck by Claudia's test tubes in particular...because I think this playful testing...let's see if I'm the wrong quality of a scientist. What is the phenomenology of science; so that you can kind of take that chemical and give it to people without them having to need the privilege of being able to pay to get a degree or know how to differentiate with respect to x. I think everyone should be able to have this feeling. In part, it's this quality of what if I was wrong. I'm ready to be wrong.

We've been helped a lot by the virus in this regard, actually. On an interpersonal level, it's terrifying, but on a larger scale, it's actually kind of benevolent in a funny way because it's forcing people to think about people they may never see in the future and time is further ahead than they have normally been thinking and planning. That's very important in itself, actually, a kind of invitation to the future, an invitation to the real actual future, a.k.a. the possibility that things can be different because what we're involved in right now is to take another virus, a very virulent, algorithmic procedure. It's called capitalism.

If Marx had access to the phrase "adaptive AI" and the concept of machine learning, he could have said, very briefly, that capitalism is an adaptive AI. The machine learns how to extract life from the biosphere without stopping.

It has no obvious logical stopping point. You actually have to switch it off or radically change it, change the code[.] So, we human beings sell our labor too cheap; that's how you make money, apparently. And then all the non-human beings actually are forced to give it away for free, and that's how it works. So, how to kind of change that? This structure that we call a building or a playground—I actually had another thought that actually it wasn't a living machine, in a way, Claudia. I was thinking it was a playmate. I was thinking what your buildings are doing, what your structures are doing, is actually transmogrifying the idea of "it's a building" into, "it's a person." I'm all in favor of making the concept of person much more readily available rather than seeing everything as a machine, which has a little bit of...everything is capable of being manipulated.

Synthetic landscapes.

If you had to choose between, let's get rid of the person-machine distinction because it's a subject-object and therefore a master-slave modality. You get rid of it, everything is a machine, in a way it still has this perfume of everything is manipulable. Whereas in a way, if everything is a person, everything is an end rather than a means to an end. We need to make this concept person slightly cheaper, not nastier, but easier for potentially every entity in the universe to have. So, got that off my chest. That was so beautiful. The idea of the building for me, from a synthetic landscapes point of view, is whatever we've been calling the building in the architecture wing, rather than landscape architecture, part of it is kind of like a crystal. This crystal is precipitating out of a solution called, in the olden days, the "landscape." In other words, what is called the "landscape" a.k.a. just the environment inevitably in social space, somewhere in history, doesn't have to be human being history, it could be the last three billion years of life on Earth. It's therefore logically prior to the building.

Funnily enough, landscape architecture shouldn't therefore be this thing that we've designed...this thing, let's put some trees around it. It should actually be the first thing that you start to think about because the entire thing, in a way, is that already. It's already an interaction with non-human beings, even if you didn't put trees around it. Your structure is already talking to non-human beings, obviously. So, how to talk to them more nicely because we're already talking to them? I was so happy to see all these algae because my examples, my reference points, are dirt for thinking about this.

A few years ago, ten years ago, R&Sie produced this hypothetical electrostatic building that I talked about a little bit in *Hyperobjects*. It's this building that sucks all of the dust from the other buildings and creates this beautiful, weirdly slightly disgusting, beautiful disgusting structure. And then you've got somebody like John Ruskin and his amazing phrase, the "Golden Stain of Time." Time is how the building is loved and caressed and cared for, deliberately or accidentally by every lifeform that touches it or walks out and brushes against it. So, this impulse of say, for example, Boris Johnson, to power wash all of the buildings in the middle of London and then put some gold on them, it's exactly the wrong attitude, I feel. And to allow buildings to be necessarily intrinsically incomplete, broken, kind of allowing them to be dirty in a way to confuse this difference, but a little bit between inside and outside. Not completely, because obviously some things are poisonous and some things are dangerous.

But this is the trouble. This is a shifting target. It's like the notion of pleasure and pain. Too much pleasure or too little pleasure equals pain. They're actually on a spectrum, like the force. The dark side of The force is just a slightly higher amplitude version of the supposedly good side of The Force. The problem of that galaxy far, far away, is that the Jedi created a hierarchical patriarchy to contain this force. So, they created this binary between the dark and the light side of the force. But as we all know, it's actually just a slightly more powerful version of the same thing.

It's the same with beauty and disgust. Slightly too much beautiful equals disgusting, slightly too much pleasure. This is going to be an aesthetic quality of the world that we build, if we build a world that actually does care for non-human beings and have non-human beings be part of social space, which they already are, but very deliberately, because beauty is going to take on a quality ever so slightly fringed with disgusting. Beauty and disgust are different, but they're going to kind of overlap because one lifeform's sense of beauty is another lifeform's disgusting.

Like a shark bites your leg off. That's, wow, that was so great. I bit this guy's leg off. From your point of view, that's this horrible nightmare that has happened to you. It can never be perfect. It can never be perfect. Imagine a being who is the most perfect master, and there's no way to serve this master properly. So, you have a thing called religion. This master is called God. That's basically what God is, some kind of master that you cannot obey properly. So, you have religion. Now imagine a servant, and this servant does exactly what you tell him to do. No more, no less with all the unintended consequences of your request. Ring any bells?

Every story you've ever heard about Satan or the fish. The fish comes out of the ocean and you have three wishes and the last wish is inevitably, "I wish you'd go back in the ocean," because life really sucks because I asked you for these wishes. In effect, Satan is the physical world. You tell the physical world to do something and it does it. You go to the supermarket and you buy an avocado from thousands and thousands of miles away. You wash your hands with antibacterial soap and you force the bacteria

Re: Action

to evolve. The biosphere does exactly what you tell it to do. No more, no less with all the unintended consequences thereof.

Therefore, doing ecological practices of any kind is literally making a deal with the devil. What is getting in the way very, very much actually, is this kind of heaven-centric idea that we have to create heaven on earth. That is actually incredibly violent, right? The name of this violence is Evangelical Christianity for the most part. American voters who actually want the world to be consumed in flames because that'll hasten the second coming of Christ.

So literally, there has to be a different approach to thinking about the biosphere that actually what is called evil and what is called the devil in so many of our implicitly platonic ways of being is actually just our physical embodiment of lifeforms inhabiting a biosphere. All of the superpowers that we have that are alienated in this kind of notion of God, including religion, morality, ethics, art, culture, all these things are coming from lifeforms. Obviously, they're coming from evolution. Many evolution theorists have all kinds of arguments about how things like religion and art come from non-human beings. I was struck by the beginning of this and I'll wrap this up by talking about the beginning of our seminar because it was said, "Have we started yet?" And this "have we started yet" quality is exactly the phenomenology of having started, period. Has global warming really started is a symptom of the fact that it started. When you are going through a totally new experience, a.k.a. trauma, the feeling of unreality is an index of the fact that it's real, that it's actually happening. This is like being in a play. At the beginning of every play there is a sense of "have we started yet" and a clever theater will play with that edge. This feeling is actually the entry into the sacred space of drama.

Now, the point about drama is that it's actually trying all the time to collapse back into dancing. If it doesn't, it's called a fascist coup on Congress and everybody knows here's the goodie, here's the baddie. The goodies going to go into Congress and kill the baddie. We have this issue. Dancing, on the other hand, more ambiguous. At the end of the play, what happens really is the audience realizes they're the lead character. The audience realizes, "Oh my God, this was all about me because I came and I got a ticket" and they wanted to see *Star Wars*. What you do is very stylized dancing called "clapping." In a comedy, of course, you also do this other kind of dancing which is an involuntary dancing called "laughing," all the way through. So, think about that, how comedy actually was always violating this implicit fourth wall that gets created by the sacred space of drama. I just want to draw your attention to the fact that this is a very interesting moment in which realizing that so-called human being audience of this spectacle is exactly what has to be gotten over. That we need to realize that human beings are based on a character in this play. And then furthermore, ultimately, the notion of goodie and baddie and the notion of beginning and conclusion, and all that needs to kind of go out the window. We're going to find ourselves in an aesthetic space that's much more ambiguous. So, anything that we can do to train the chicken, to tolerate ambiguity is going to be a fundamental component of an expanded version of democracy, which is what is required. Thank you.

HR   Timothy, thank you. That was fascinating, and you certainly covered so many vectors and exciting points that each one of them could spawn many paragraphs. I have a question because you instantly converted me to another way of thinking about the proverbial chicken egg and AI potentiality. Perhaps this is a contentious statement because AI is more often than not portrayed as potentially evil. If you say that Satan is at work all the time and that we are, in fact, in a kind of pact with it and signed on to a silent contract, is AI then potentially our soon-to-be new replacement nature? By that, I mean that it takes on the other side of what you are talking about, even though we spend all our time worrying that AI will summon all the evil that we see in all the films that portray it. Is AI some demonic force that will take over and eventually kill all humankind and control everything, or is there another potential future at work?

TM   I don't understand some of the terms and frames of reference, but I can say that this is not a talk that is opposing the concept of artificial intelligence. I'm trying to describe capitalism and what it does. It's an algorithm they call procedure. What is wrong with AI in that respect is not so much the "I." Once you've determined that "I" is A, then basically you've decided that all kinds of "I" are already "A." That's not the problem. The problem is the automation. The problem is switching something on and watching it running and going, "Hmm, I wonder how much biosphere this is going to munch down before I remember that I'm in charge of this machine? Or am I just going to tolerate it doing that until we're all dead or more dead, much more dead than we are?"

HR   What I'm getting at, can AI in fact be the antidote? Can it, in fact, work in the opposite direction?

TM   It's too much. It's too broad and I can't answer that question. I'm sorry.

HR   An exciting aspect of what was clearly articulated by you is the notion of a building being a sort of "crystal" set within the landscape being an insertion into a lifeform. I think there is a rich history in our discipline of this concept. I am thinking of architects and visionaries such as Italian Paolo Soleri and the Austrian-American Friedrich Kiesler, the work of the American architect Bruce Goff and especially Hermann Finsterlin, the great German visionary. These and some other historically relevant figures were indeed prescient people that intuited the sorts of relationships you speak of. These individuals were very far out there on the periphery of our discipline. They are often thought of as strange and marginal characters. However, they are all more pertinent today than they were in their lifetimes. These are the ideas and figures that one today should study deeply.

It is an exciting equation to consider that we as architects should and must be working at the service of nature. That reminds me a little bit of the children's game we all played where one puts a string into a liquid of saturated sugar and watches beautiful crystals form. Architecture is, therefore, an outcome of our limited understanding of nature, especially nature as a dominant force, not something we should oppose or attempt to always control.

TM   I try as hard as I can to never say the word "nature." I wrote this book called *Ecology without Nature*, and the reason why is that I think this concept has really been deemed toxic actually. I prefer to say biosphere because it's real. How does it work? It works through evolution and symbiosis, which are also real or at least science says they're true, and that's about as true as we can get now.

HR   We will move on to the third speaker today, Anab Jain. She is a designer, futurist, filmmaker, and educator, having received a Master's in Interactive Design at the Royal College of Art in London and has a broad range of experience from her role as an executive producer for documentary films such as *Journeys* to various positions through the 2000s as an experienced interaction designer with a wide range of companies and organizations such as advertising from MRM, McCann WorldGroup...as well as Helen Hanlon Research Centre, the Royal College of Art, where she undertook a design and research for future escapes of work and finally, the position as a senior interaction designer in Nokia and Microsoft.

In 2009, Anab founded Superflux along with Jon Ardern. Superflux is a boundary-defying award-winning design experimental futures group and a research and art practice. Its mission is to investigate the complexities of our rapidly changing technological landscapes and the social, political, economic, and cultural implications of such changes. From climate change to algorithmic autonomy, future of work to more-than-human politics, the work of Superflux aims to confront diverse audiences with the complex and deeply interconnected nature of the challenges facing us today.

Re: Action

For their ten-years-plus contribution to the field of speculative future design and their committed social mission, Superflux received the Design Studio of the Year Award in 2021. Anab Jain, as a professor of Design Investigations at the Angewandte, aims to realize the vision of a studio as a new kind of design practice responsive to the challenges and opportunities of the 21st century, that builds on individual and collective experiences and interests to foster open-ended politically critical and socially relevant creative positions. Anab, it is a great pleasure to have you here with us today, please, if you will, take the Zoom floor.

Anab Jain Thank you. Thanks, Hani. Those were great talks. I'm not sure how I'll follow up, but I can see I'm not going to talk about architecture. I'm not an architect. I want to start with a shameless plug of my students. Our course at the Angewandte is called "Design Investigations." We are a part of industrial design. Please go and check out our Instagram and our website. They are doing a lot of exciting work.
My own studio practice is Superflux. We are a bunch of various artists, designers, makers, technologists based in London and we do projects that imagine and experiment with alternate speculative planetary worlds that celebrate ecological resurgence. Today...I wanted to really touch on some kind of meta-frames and guiding principles that...frame a lot of our practice at Superflux. I'm going to start by reading out a phrase, a bunch of paragraphs from a book.

O eastern light, awaken Those who have slept! The darkness will be broken, The promise kept.

It is our suffering that brings us together. It is not love. Love does not obey the mind, and turns to hate when forced. The bond that binds us is beyond choice. We are brothers. We are brothers in what we share. In pain, which each of us must suffer alone, in hunger, in poverty, in hope, we know our brotherhood. We know it, because we have had to learn it. We know that there is no help for us but from one another, that no hand will save us if we do not reach out our hand. And the hand that you reach out is empty, as mine is. You have nothing. You possess nothing. You own nothing. You are free. All you have is what you are, and what you give.

I am here because you see in me the promise, the promise that we made two hundred years ago in this city—the promise kept. We have kept it, on Anarres. We have nothing but our freedom. We have nothing to give you but your own freedom. We have no law but the single principle of mutual aid between individuals. We have no government but the single principle of free association. We have no states, no nations, no presidents, no premiers, no chiefs, no generals, no bosses, no bankers, no landlords, no wages, no charity, no police, no soldiers, no wars. Nor do we have much else. We are sharers, not owners. We are not prosperous. None of us is rich. None of us is powerful. If it is Anarres you want, if it is the future you seek, then I tell you that you must come to it with empty hands. You must come to it alone, and naked, as the child comes into the world, into his future, without any past, without any property, wholly dependent on other people for his life. You cannot take what you have not given, and you must give yourself. You cannot buy the Revolution. You cannot make the Revolution. You can only be the Revolution. It is in your spirit, or it is nowhere.

ambiguous utopia

I want to talk about the fact that all design practice, all artistic practice, all architecture is political. We can only be the revolution in the work we're trying to do. This is a quote from Ursula K. Le Guin's book *The Dispossessed*. For those of you who don't know, Le Guin wrote *The Dispossessed* about an "ambiguous utopia," as she calls it. It resonates a lot with me. Basically, the question is, "What does it mean in today's context, when you say you can only be the revolution?" I'm asking that of myself, but I'm also asking of all of us here, and I want to explore briefly what that might look like.

Perhaps to me, it feels a bit like a calling. It's a time when perhaps we need to ask these questions. I'll try and connect that to some of the works we do. This book is about a young man's journey across two opposing planets and societies—one anarchistic-communistic and the other capitalistic-repressive—in search of his own identity, political freedom, and justice. Le Guin used the concept of opposites to really write about two different planets and societies. Anarres is an anarchist society governed by principles free from state rule, while Urras is a capitalist regime and appears to be utopian.

Le Guin created the planet Anarres intending to promote what she deemed to be new ideas, where water and heat should be rationed, when nothing goes to waste. When I started thinking about what I'd share today...I dug into why she wrote this book a bit more. She said she was actually really unhappy when she started writing it. She needed to understand—she said:

> *My own passionate opposition to the war that we are in endlessly seemed raging in Vietnam, and endlessly protesting at home. If I had known that, that my country would continue making aggressive wars for the rest of my life, I might have had less energy for protesting that one. But knowing only that I didn't want to study war no more. I studied peace. I started by reading a whole mess of utopias and learning something on pacifism, and Gandhi and nonviolent resistance.*

She continued to say, "This led me to the nonviolent anarchist writers such as Peter Kropotkin and Paul Goodman. With them I find a great affinity. They enabled me to think about war, peace, politics, and how we go with one another and ourselves and the value of failure and the strength of what is weak." We know very well now that this book by Peter Kropotkin became so kind of valuable, let's say in the pandemic, where mutually groups were formed everywhere all across the world, my own course, we formed a mutual aid group then.

Now with the horrific war in Ukraine we are witnessing, I'm trying to make a case for the fact that none of this is outside of architectural design and artistic practices. These things that are happening all around us matter and our practices and instruments we use to create our practices matter more than ever before. According to Kropotkin, it was not love and not even sympathy upon which society is based in mankind. It's the conscience, but only at that stage do humans have an instinct of solidarity. The incredible amount of support that people who have had to flee Ukraine have received is really deeply moving.

But unfortunately, as I look around me, this form of human solidarity is not a singular reality. Today, the nature of crisis is way too difficult, exacerbated by the device of information landscape. The information landscape is immersed in an alternate fictional reality. Propaganda reigns supreme. Our ability to make sense of it all is compounded with the life challenges of climate crisis, global warming, conditions that have led to a collective sense of anxiety, discord, anger, disenfranchisement.

It's times like these that I once again draw inspiration from Le Guin to underwrite the kind of revolution we all need to be part of. Even Cameron wrote once that Le Guin's work was built on a foundation that the human soul's capacity for stoic and principle resistance to oppression was indistinguishable. I believe that Le Guin's revolution is one that resides in all of us.

> *"We live in capitalism; its power seems inescapable. So did the divine right of kings. Any human power can be resisted and changed by human beings.*
> *Resistance and change often begin in art and very often in our art, the art of words."*
> *— Ursula Le Guin (1929–2018)*

I'd like to call it stoic and principle resistance: the positions, the perspectives and attitudes we adapt and adopt to relate with the complexities around us as critical activism. What I have been doing is trying to create a lexicon, a work in progress very much, a lexicon for the practice of critical activism. A lexicon that helps us switch perspectives from the capitalist modernity that we're trapped in towards precarious flourishing. To understand, as actually Timothy Morton just said, "making the deal with the devil," conditions and principles that help us disentangle ourselves from the grips of capitalism, and one that makes us believe that there are no alternatives, that there can be no other way of living towards a framework that helps us imagine what it might be to flourish, as honesty ignites amid precarity, uncertainty, and instability. From uncompromising dogma towards guiding principles, from a desire to certainty towards contingent possibilities, from the unnecessary focus on being right, knowing everything towards nurturing and embracing doubt, being okay with not knowing all the answers, being okay when others say they don't know. From maximizing value, actually attempts that the present modernist ambitions to control. In contrast, emergence sustainability. Transformation is built on values of care, for the privileges of interdependence, egalitarianism. Care that promotes social and ecological justice through solidarity and collective action. From governance to cooperation, from this idea of limitless human progress to ecological researchers, from singular grand narratives to emergent mythologies, and what those emergent mythologies could be.

At Superflux, in the last couple of years, three projects come to mind that are stories of care, cooperation, humility and solidarity, interdependence and renewal that explore these principles. I'm not going to go deep into each of them, but really touch upon them. For instance, the idea of the intersection emerged from an applied project that asked us to imagine hopeful futures around democratic technologies. Technologies that are currently extracted in nature, technologies that are ever present, always on, barreling us with every single interaction towards more extraction and exploitation. What does, in this context, a hopeful and positive future look like?

When we were doing this work, this happened: the tragic murderers of Breonna Taylor and George Floyd, the related protests, the swelling moment of Black Lives Matter, the emergence of QAnon, the global COVID pandemic, US elections, the heat, the fires, the wildfires in Australia etc. These all became the scope of the project. I ran across the work of Ashish Ghadiali, who really further firmed up things we were discovering, that:

> *understanding the roots of climate change means understanding the 500-year history of slavery, of colonialism, of neoliberal structural adjustment, as part of one continuous narrative. Only by recognizing the multiple connections between these seeds of oppression, can we start to create a community of care around the world.*
> — Ashish Ghadiali, filmmaker and climate activist

We've built this fifteen-minute documentary inspired by Ken Burns, *Ministry of Dust*, to talk the journey through four protagonists. Each of them move through really turbulent movements, like this journalist whose work was diluted by AI systems into a peak economy, pay-per-click writing job. A disillusioned hardware engineer's techno-utopian dreams are shattered by the realization the tech companies extract from us the same way oil companies extract from the planet. A young climate migrant who became a refugee in her own country. It's called "The Intersection." The story eventually is a journey from a wide present to a cooperative future, telling stories of active hope for those who have fought to reimagine extractive technology to serve community, support nature, and value planetary relationships.

[V]   I've been in this fight for as long as I can remember. Everyone out in the streets like it was the last option we had. Our message was simple. We were fighting for justice, but somehow it got twisted. Out of all this chaos we built something.

AJ   There was a viewing guide. We created tools for the protagonist from the waste of the Anthropocene—a term that we are calling the "Craftocene"—speculative artifacts that propose alternate craft manifestations of technology and move into smaller and tightly communities. Imagine decentralized mesh networks and celebrate the connection between technology and our biospheres.

This is a server by frame that was a nomadic storage device for transporting and sharing data...a sensor network and EBE Inkbase device which gathers and visualizes data, hyperlocal mesh network, sensing nodes, along with a bunch of principles that emerge from non-extractive diversity, kinship with the land we live with, and so on. These are principles akin to the work we were doing otherwise, beautifully written in the book *Overstory* by Richard Powers: "There are no individuals in the forest, no separable events. The bird and the branch it sits on, a joint thing. A third or more of the food a big tree makes goes to feed other organisms. Even different kinds of trees form partnerships. Cut down a birch, and a nearby Douglas fir may suffer[.]"

So here we were trying to draw connections between technology, the climate crisis, and our relationship to the land and themes of kinship, themes of love and care, mutual aid and solidarity, to extend the idea of solidarity to other ecologies we share our planet with. Really, the question that emerged alongside the work we were doing was, "Can we become more forest?" That led to the work we did for the MAK, the Museum of Applied Arts, at the Vienna Biennale, called *Invocation for Hope*, in which we were looking at monoculture growth and the idea of human-exerted control over nature, the fire and black forest that serve as a cynical note before anthropogenic climate change as a whole. This is a wildfire that happened in Austria's Neunkirchen region. We collaborated with the forest department and fire department to salvage four hundred fire-blackened, burned trees and bring them to the MAK and invited visitors to meander past the skeletal remains of the black pine. Millennia of communicable bonds broken by human greed. Holy ecologies destroyed by capitalism and war, destroying life-sustaining towards human and non-human alike. We invited visitors to hold on to this predicament and continue the journey as they hear the whispers of his primary frond, unfurling in the mythic shadows of black-burned pine. "Come along with abandon," we said, "and embrace the spirit of renewal amongst damaged ruins." In the heart of a death forest, a glimpse of interdependent, tentacular flourishing: multiple different species, mosses, grasses, lichens, shrubs, all growing symbiotically over the course of the installation. When you look in the pond, you see a reflection of yourself or of another species inviting contemplation: what is our space? What does it mean to be human in a more-than-human world? Worlds where humans and non-humans carve and shape their destinies together. A spellbinding chorus created by Cosmo Sheldrake invited visitors to go on a personal journey, from the ravages of climate crisis, the possibility of renewal. That kind of work was about generating this idea for more-than-human politics, which gives us new opportunities to imagine care, humility, imagination, interdependence, resistance, reward and mourning.

This is the kind of thinking that led us to create the work *Refuge for Researchers*, shown at the Venice Biennale early last year and at the Barbican in London next week, actually. It's a multi-species banquet, inviting fourteen different species, including pests and vermin, to dine together, a kind of cross-section of life and resurgence. They all sit and dine in this deconstructed home of a man and woman and a child joins a fox, a rat, a wasp, pigeon, a cow, a wild boar, a snake, a beaver, a wolf, a raven, and a mushroom. The scene lays bare conversation between the paralysis of fear and the audacity of hope. Species ceremonially crafted cutlery. This is the wild boar, a patron of sea dispersal and resilience. The shard of a broken record is attached to a lichen-covered branch. A small celebration of multi symbiosis. The wasp scoop honey dipper and feather brush are constructed using jewelry-making processes. Overall, the journey invited visitors to consider a move from patriarchy to matriarchy. A wilder rewilding, more or less mythological, perhaps a more real urge for a world that is built upon sediments—where we are today—but imagining a wild world where essentially the idea, it was like a prayer actually...

[V]   The world is changing in unison with one another. In unison with the changing climate... The dance of life having and slowing across time.

AJ   This was a whole poem that was also recited outside of soundscape for this multi species banquet. So, coming back to the idea of precarious flourishing where human conceit is not the only plan for making worlds, what sort of world-making projects emerge from our entanglement with other species from our intentional, practical activities? Thank you, and thank you to all the people who've played a key role in realizing the work that we've been doing the last couple of years. Thank you.

BITBIOBOT by ecoLogicStudio (© Marco Cappelletti)

Automated Traffic Surveillance and Control (ATSAC) Center (Photo Courtesy of LADOT)

166   Panel Talk: Corrective Methodologies and Architectural Futures

HR Thank you, that was really very beautiful and very profound. It makes me think a lot about the blind belief we have in innovation and progress, which we certainly put into question. We have to, unfortunately given the time, move right to Greg. Greg Lynn has a remarkable and international reputation as an innovator in redefining the medium of design and digital technology as well as pioneering the fabrication and manufacture of complex functional and ergonomic forms using computers, numerically controlled machinery and technologies.

Greg is a professor here at the University of Applied Arts Vienna. He is also a professor at UCLA and has held many academic positions worldwide. He is a principal of Greg Lynn FORM, an LA-based architecture and design practice, has been included in numerous publications, and had many academic writings published. Greg Lynn FORM has been influential in the acceptance of advanced materials and technologies for design, fabrication, and design opportunities to extend across multiple scales and media. Greg's studio continues to define what was considered the cutting edge of design in various fields. Greg has also designed consumer products utilizing materials and manufacturing technologies with companies like Vitra, Alessi, Nike, and most recently, Swarovski. He is also co-founder and chief creative officer of the Boston-based intelligent light mobility company Piaggio Fast Forward. Greg has worked in various permanent collections at museums worldwide, including the CCA in Montreal, CF San Francisco, MoMA, ICA Chicago, and the mumok here in Vienna.

Greg received the American Academy of Arts and Letters Award in 2001 and 2003. TIME magazine named Greg one of the 100 most innovative people in the world for the 21st century, and Forbes magazine named him one of the ten most influential living artists in 2008. Greg won the Golden Lion at the 11th Venice Biennale in 2010. Greg also co-represented the United States at the 2006 Venice Biennale with me. Greg, it is great to have you here. The floor is yours.

Greg Lynn Thanks Hani, that's very kind and I feel like I may be at risk of being the voice of blind enthusiasm for innovation, but please take everything I'm going to show you with a degree of cynicism and mostly challenge.

I brought some images, just to start a conversation. I didn't bring any of my own work or the students' work. Instead, I thought I would pose a few of the challenges that we all are facing in the field of architecture. As architects, we love and care for our clients and we want to do the best job we can for them. If we're being honest, our primary responsibility is to think beyond a client and design to improve the civic realm. There aren't that many professions left concerned with what it is to be a citizen and what spaces citizens need in order to live and work and flourish together. Architecture is one of the last places where job one is thinking about what it is to be a citizen of the world, in a city, and in your daily life. So, everything I'm going to show describes challenges for us to think about regarding civic life.

The first image is of the ATSAC or Automated Traffic Surveillance and Control System, in Los Angeles that was developed for the 1984 Olympics. It remains one of the most sophisticated traffic intelligence technologies on Earth. It allows the LA Department of Transportation to instantly shut down streets for protests or create what they call street parks where they'll close down traffic and move street furniture in. It's a very sophisticated and powerful tool. It has surveillance in the title, but its primary function is to manage the flows of pedestrians, buses, automobiles, bicycles, etc. This is a form of urbanism that's extremely powerful. If you want to talk about civic space, it's one of the tools used to create civic space in Los Angeles currently.

The next slide is a view of what ATSAC sees. This is Exposition Park, one of the most populated parks in Los Angeles in a very diverse neighborhood. What you're seeing are the control systems for monitoring traffic, opening and closing streets, controlling streetlights and their syncopation.

In the next image, you see what transportation is becoming. It's riding with a stranger in their leased car from Uber. What you notice is most Uber drivers drive Toyota Camry models because that's what Uber recommends that their drivers lease and insure from them. This is a case, not unlike taxi and delivery where a private company is deploying their business within public infrastructure. What you're going to see for the next several slides is what's happening more and more frequently, which is that companies are figuring out

Re: Action

how to build a business on public sidewalks and streets. I live in Venice Beach, which is ground zero for every new idea about transportation. Venice Beach, on a weekend, is the most populated public space in the United States, with over two million visitors per day. Tourists come to Venice or Santa Monica to have the experience of riding on a rented push scooter and updating their social media on their phones while they ride. This is part of the tourist experience economy. It's also replacing walking.

You can see that people are spending more and more time on their telephones while walking in towns and cities, either navigating, looking for a mural to take their picture in front of, or communicating with their friends. This is another challenge for civic spaces. You can design a space for human interaction and then people get there and have their faces in their phones, interacting with each other remotely on screens. One might even describe it as citizens broadcasting remotely with video feeds from their phones. The amount of screen time that a person spends now is just astonishing when you think about work time on screen, leisure time on screen, and transportation time on screen.

In the next image, what's happening now in terms of transportation infrastructure, with a lot of cities closing to automobiles, you're seeing a sharing economy of electric bicycles, electric scooters, and ride hailing. There is little planning, design or legislation regarding how these devices and vehicles get parked, charged, repositioned, and maintained.

Next image is what now is the latest addition to sidewalks, parks, plazas, campuses and bicycle lanes and that is land drones. With the exception of robots deployed on pedestrian college campuses, 100% of these are driven by remote control by gig workers looking through computer monitors using joysticks. These robots are now everywhere in Santa Monica and Venice where they are able to pilot while the cities determine legislative policy. It's like each one is on its own little Mars mission to deliver a burrito or bowl. It is an example of an incredible technology and labor initiative to try to bring services and food to people who now instead of going out to eat in restaurants, prefer to eat at home and have food delivered. These delivery services, by robot or Uber driver, are supported by vast cloud kitchens or local ghost kitchens where one or dozens of restaurants will all operate out of the same kitchen, where there's nowhere to sit and eat. By the way that goes, it trends more towards fairly expensive food offerings.
This aerial view of a street during COVID restrictions mandating outdoor dining is linked with current initiatives to pedestrianized cities. During COVID, shopping and dining moved outdoors. Many people want to adopt this pedestrian claim of parking spaces and roadways permanently.

The next image is to make the point that there is a mandate towards electrification that's going on with automobiles as well as delivery vans and trucks. Linked with the simplification of electric vehicles and the greater expense of electric vehicles due to their drivetrain is a desire to make it attractive to spend more time in automobiles and exploit their use for more hours of the day. This desire for more intensive and extensive use of cars is not driven primarily by sustainability. The move towards autonomous automobiles is to make longer commutes more viable and more time and automobiles more acceptable.

The last image I'll show you is that it is not an accident that self-driving technology was first initiated by Apple and Google. The average American spends thirty-seven minutes each way commuting in a private car and given the opportunity to get seventy-four minutes a day of people's eyeballs in a closed cabin where they can control all of the content, meaning that you're watching 100% Apple content through an Apple device.

These are all the challenges we address in my studio here at the Angewandte and in my professional office. These are the challenges that change the game in terms of civic space and they all have spatial consequences.

HR Thank you, Greg. Fantastic and, as always, and strangely, disconcerting.

GL   Sorry, I did mean to be optimistic as these are all new problems and therefore new opportunities.

HR   What I mean by disconcerting is that in contrast to the other presentations, I see from your talk that four distinct vectors are emerging for the near future. Moreover, each is remarkably unique and intriguing. They all seem to point to a convergence ultimately on a notion of the necessity of our seriously questioning innovation. Also, the idea of embracing obsolescence and understanding our relationship to the biosphere is a pact that we need to reconsider. And then there is this idea of remedy, which I found curious, especially in Claudia's work.

So, if I were to put a question to close, I would ask you all to make brief closing statements. I will point out that the proverbial embellished elephant in the room is indeed architecture as we know it today. I think that that is interesting and quite profound. In other words, the question of the re-relevancy of our discipline.

So, do we need to continue to innovate and create potentially problematic futures? Much of what we talked about and saw today, which was beautifully expressed, was perhaps that we do not need to maintain a preoccupation with technological innovation and streamlining.

These vectors discussed today are the notion of working symbiotically with obsolescence, our discovering and awakening to a newfound co-relationship with the biosphere, the making of architecture and spatiality as a form of remedy and repair, and above all, the idea that innovation and progress are not a means in and of themselves are all profoundly compelling. These are four wildly attractive conceptual turbulences that aligned beautifully today. Are there any concluding remarks? I think we can start with Greg.

GL   I always rush towards any form of progress. It has more to do with character than intelligence. I know for my robotics company, we saw what was happening with delivery, with services, and said, "Our competitors are bird scooters and ride hailing because people don't walk." People will rent a scooter to go as little as five hundred meters. The average time you spend in a ride-hailing car in the United States is under two miles on average. All of that's walkable.

So, we designed a robot that has the intelligence of a weapon being used in Ukraine right now, but pointed at the target of helping people be more mobile and connected with the world without ever needing to look at a screen while moving with a piece of very high technology. It has a single button, and it is so intuitive, even a two-year-old can use it without any explanation. It's meant to help people walk around and socialize, to be present in their communities again so they're not on their phones all the time. They're seeing the local shops, they're seeing familiar strangers, much like you do when you walk a dog. People are more aware and engaged.

For me, the screen is the biggest problem for the built environment, not to mention an initiative to build a Metaverse. This is deeply problematic to me. Every design decision I make is how do I avoid having a screen involved and how can I help people to be aware of each other and their environment. Right now, this is not where the action is and I realize I am being counter to most people's assumptions about how to be innovative.

HR   No pun intended, but that is an exciting segue to Anab's work because I cannot imagine anything more antithetical to what Greg just described than having an actual fox having dinner next to you. Would you like to add something, Anab?

AJ   Maybe just a couple of things that stuck in my mind: the idea of designers and architects in this instance, the idea of the final object or the final building, or the final solution. So the word "solution" was problematic, meaning the singular object or singular building as the solution. I think we need to move away from both of those kinds of ideas. If we are to, quote-unquote, "progress" in that world it is problematic.

Re: Action

So, I would suggest to look for solutions in the problems actually because with every solution comes the problem. With designers who are designing things for solutions, as Lebbeus Woods once said, "You are the problem." We are the problem here as much as anything else.

I think, to think of relationality we always think of the final object, the building, the product, the thing. But the space in between is where the exciting stuff is happening, between the two things. I would consider us to think about those in between spaces and those relationalities a bit more.

HR That leads us to Timothy. Timothy, any further remarks on the biosphere?

You mentioned today that we are not on the verge of global warming or massive change; instead, this is utterly erroneous because we are in the middle of these situations.

TM I want to very much go on record as categorically opposing the idea that innovation is the problem. I heard Anab talking about innovating a whole new way of coexisting together in social space, and I heard Claudia talking about innovating wonderful structures that don't suck. So, the problem is not innovation. The problem is actually precisely the opposite, which is allowing an automated system, which at its largest scale is called capitalism to keep going without stopping. Precisely, the problem is not to do with innovation. Heavens, I mean, we need to be more creative and more playful, a.k.a. we need to invite the future to be different than the past.

One of the things about Google, I've talked to Google a couple of times. As a kind of dissident faction in Google that's not keen on what Google is doing, I talk to them sometimes. One of the things about them and a lot of tech companies is that they're all about a kind of serious playfulness, that is the weaponized, as you said, a military rise to deployment of playful things. Whereas what we actually need, of course, is playful seriousness, a.k.a. the playful deployment of extremely profound and serious ideas. I found Anab and Claudia to be articulating precisely those.

HR Very nice. Claudia, did you want to elaborate on that or closing remarks?

CP Well, yes, sometimes when I talk to my students, I suggest that a key remit of architecture is not solving problems but re-problematizing them from a new perspective. This is not because we don't want to solve practical problems but because it is important to see them in a different manner or simply interact with them to expand the space of possible solutions. This applies for example to the current climate emergency. You can't deal creatively with an emergency while you see it as such. I feel we simply need to start looking, feeling, smelling, growing and finally as a consequence transforming the planet we are part of.

HR Timothy, you brought me back to a memory of when I started teaching here at the Angewandte almost a decade ago. The first psychologically motivated "move" I made was to territorialize my space. Moreover, I did that with a massive Lawrence Weiner-inspired wordplay just above the studio entrance. "Serious Fun" was posted there as a mantra to inspire and take over the school.

All five of us together today, and mainly the four of you, showed us each of your relentless and intelligent pursuits of serious fun. With that, I want to thank you all for taking the time to talk with us today and being part of this studio's trajectory going forward.

The students, I am sure, were very, very inspired today. Now I have much damage control to do, but that's okay. It's a good thing. Thanks a lot, and Greg and Anab, I look forward to seeing you around the school. Claudia and Timothy, it would be fantastic to have you with us at the school to look at the students' work. Thank you so much to my teaching staff and assistants for putting all this together. It has been a brilliant morning, afternoon, and evening for some of you. We will see you all soon and hope to talk again. I think with that we will close up.

Refuge for Resurgence by Superflux at Droog (© Thijs Wolzak)

EC(O)CENTRIC FORM

Lenia Mascha

ACTIONS OF DISCOVERY

Embarking on a journey to discover new forms of architecture is probably one of the most exciting acts in architectural education and professional practice. Whether one sets sail searching for ideas, searching for answers to specific questions, or simply maneuvering on the vast sea of speculation, a world of endless shapes and architectural possibilities awaits. In this form-seeking experience, encounters might prove invaluable, and the joy of a single discovery can be deeply rewarding. Architectural education and design research should safeguard this privilege of time and training for such a daring act. Most of all, because such journeys and findings have the power to transform one's stance toward the discipline, sometimes even to transform the discipline itself.

A future-oriented pedagogy sets off such architectural expeditions toward uncharted territories. Every voyage contributes to the mapping and expanding of the limits of the known morphological worldview. What paths, challenges, and new destinations lie ahead? Which emerging forms will prove to be timeless and which will turn obsolete in the years to come? How will they change the dominant paradigms of the present, and how, if possible at all, can these architectural gestures contribute to foreseeing and shaping the future? A solid pedagogical agenda offers a significant advantage to architects by orienting their formal expeditions in prosperous directions. Such an agenda equips architects with both thinking and practicing tools to navigate confidently in the face of a fluctuating and sometimes turbulent weather forecast.

ACTIONS OF THE WEATHER

Today, the seas are stormy. Since the turn of the century, the accelerated pace at which our political, environmental, technological, and human conditions are developing and the ripple effects of world-changing crises and sequenced unprecedented disruptions have led to the normalization of a state of agitation and flux, shock, and uncertainty. The convergence of financial, humanitarian, migratory, sanitary, and environmental emergencies is today more exposed and evident than before, mainly due to our increasingly interconnected world. To understand and exit this vicious cycle, the need to act becomes urgent.

Actions of aid and repair are vital and can offer comfort and temporary, or sometimes permanent, resolutions, even if such acts address the consequences and not the cause of events. On the other hand, efforts to fix and resolve a crisis might seem way more necessary, yet again extremely hard to define. And that is because there are crises where no action seems bold enough to succeed. Those are the crises we can't adequately address, we can't fix, and we can't remain unaffected by them. That is because today, we are witnessing an anomaly of the dominant paradigms that can be documented, confirmed, and deeply felt. It can be measured in the record high summer temperatures of the planet, in the rising waters of the oceans, in the accelerated melting of polar glaciers and shaken optimism of everyone that hasn't been paying much attention.

Global warming is here to stay. What has been long underrated as far-away trouble and a seasonal "change" of weather patterns reveals itself as a raging fire, heat, drought, and flood. Today, every inhabited region across the planet is already affected by the climate crisis and extreme weather.[1] The Intergovernmental Panel for Climate Change (IPCC) assesses that global temperatures will continue to increase under all emission scenarios (even the most optimistic ones) until at least the mid-century, mainly due to the irreparable human-induced harm already caused to the environment.[2] Weather extremes and climate shocks will occur more frequently and become more severe. And with every increment of global warming caused by today's actions (or environmental inaction), the projected adverse impacts and related hazards to the ecosystem will only escalate.[3] If no rapid, drastic, and forceful actions are taken, present and future generations will be in critical danger.

A visionary architecture looks forward into the future. Yet none of its futures can exist on a dead planet. How can architects plan, design, speculate and be visionary in times of climate calamities and extreme conditions? How can architectural pedagogies defend creativity, playfulness, and intuition when their actual processes are disrupted by the outbreaks of pandemics, wars, and extreme weather phenomena? And if we do want to embark on a journey of morphological investigation, how can we sail on these rising and turbulent waters that our human world at its core is so violently stirring?

ACTIONS OF AWARENESS

While postwar architecture has celebrated the value of culture as an act of progress-driven optimism toward a better future, today this sense of confidence is on the line. Speaking of optimism during a fire emergency might seem like a questionable survival strategy at first glance. Nevertheless, awareness can be an invaluable environmental act. Paradigm shifts, understood through the philosophical lens of Thomas Kuhn, the man who popularized the term, are driven by the (otherwise very dark) revelation of an unresolved crisis and the evident malfunctioning of the dominant paradigms; this awareness, according to Kuhn's paradigm theory is the prelude to revolutionary ideas and an indication of an emerging paradigm change and the retooling of the discipline.[4] A future-oriented pedagogy always lies in wait for such indications. This readiness allows a timely disciplinary response to the ideas and events that foster change in the world.

Shifting the focus to today's most pressing challenges is also an essential pedagogical act. It doesn't only contribute to training tomorrow's architects, it also cultivates a spirit of active civic conscience through targeted information-gathering, thematic investigation, historical and scientific field research, the collection and analysis of data and facts, and their interpretation. It encourages articulating concerns, opinions, and positions toward contemporary phenomena. It's an educational process that inspires ideas and concepts of world-changing actions that can be hypothesized, tested, studied, and discussed among peers.

Awareness brings further shifts in terminology. Words such as climate "change" stand weak once realizing the anthropogenic harm to ecosystems and the mass extinction of species. In this sense, climate "crisis" and "emergency" emphasize better the urgency for action. Environmental equity and social justice become inseparable aspects of ecological thinking. Decarbonization requires decolonizing the relationships with nature and history. The act of caring becomes a significant act of intelligence. The call for "sustainable development," a widespread term for public and private stakeholders, gains a more profound meaning when used in the context of democratic values, intercultural expression, biodiversity, human rights, and animal rights. The emphasis on globalization and technological progress (and in the architectural context, the role of the global architect and tech pioneer) expands to an even larger scale that requires planetary thinking, ecological awareness, and collective aspirations. Anthropocentrism passes the stage to ecocentrism, an inclusive term for all life forms and ecosystems, and the praise of individuality loses ground in favor of eco-dependence.

ACTIONS OF ECCENTRICITY AND ECOCENTRISM

So, what happens to the journey of form-discovery? Does it still make sense to depart? Can it still be valuable, rewarding, worth taking? Is it naive, superficial, eccentric? Is it considered, under this extreme weather forecast, dangerous or disorienting?

Revisiting Thomas Kuhn's arguments can help justify a rigorous response. In his words, "to reject one paradigm without simultaneously substituting another is to reject science itself."[5] A visionary practice has always explored this analogy in architecture. Because without working on discovering the architectural ideas and forms that will replace the systems, programs, rules, and premises that are being rejected as obsolete, climate-damaging, and future-threatening, one can feel immediately lost and question the discipline itself. Vision, imagination, creativity, and storytelling are the ideal places to pursue new methods that can substitute what is now not working. A forward-thinking architectural education plays a pivotal role in enacting such visions. It has the power to empower, inspire and direct the energy and focus of tomorrow's practitioners to invent a positive future. In an open pedagogical framework of design research at the intersection of art and science, of hypotheses and aspirations, architects can critically engage with and freely immerse in the acts of imagining, examining, and articulating alternative, desired scenarios that override the predicted ones. These actions are both eccentric and ecocentric in essence, as they deviate from an established center of thinking and orbit beyond a world in crisis, around a world of ecological importance.

1   "IPCC, 2021: Summary for Policymakers," in: Climate Change 2021: The Physical Science Basis. Contribution of Working Group I to the Sixth Assessment Report of the Intergovernmental Panel on Climate Change, [Masson-Delmotte, V., P. Zhai, A. Pirani, S.L. Connors, C. Péan, S. Berger, N. Caud, Y. Chen, L. Goldfarb, M.I. Gomis, M. Huang, K. Leitzell, E. Lonnoy, J.B.R. Matthews, T.K. Maycock, T. Waterfield, O. Yelekçi, R. Yu, and B. Zhou (eds.)], (Cambridge, United Kingdom and New York, NY, USA: Cambridge University Press, 2021), p. 10.
2   Ibid. 14
3   "IPCC, 2022: Summary for Policymakers," [H.-O. Pörtner, D.C. Roberts, E.S. Poloczanska, K. Mintenbeck, M. Tignor, A. Alegría, M. Craig, S. Langsdorf, S. Löschke, V. Möller, A. Okem (eds.)] in: Climate Change 2022: Impacts, Adaptation, and Vulnerability. Contribution of Working Group II to the Sixth Assessment Report of the Intergovernmental Panel on Climate Change, [H.-O. Pörtner, D.C. Roberts, M. Tignor, E.S. Poloczanska, K. Mintenbeck, A. Alegría, M. Craig, S. Langsdorf, S. Löschke, V. Möller, A. Okem, B. Rama (eds.)], (Cambridge, United Kingdom: Cambridge University Press, in press), p. 18.
4   Thomas S. Kuhn, *The Structure of Scientific Revolutions*, (Chicago: The University of Chicago Press, 2012), p. 76.
5   Kuhn, *The Structure of Scientific Revolutions*, p. 79.

Re: Resilience

Sophie Luger

Studio Hani Rashid has been focusing on developing an architecture that responds to the current and future ecological changes in our environment as well as social and political topics since it was established in 2011. Whether it was to develop prototypes for a future city or to look at Antarctica's current ecological crisis, the studio was always driven by an incredible motivation and eagerness by all members of the studio to address these topics in a profound but also very much-needed lighthearted way. By the time this book was under "construction," our comfortable, secure, and seemingly robust western world had changed. The climate emergency became more evident than ever. A pandemic forced everyone to retreat into their homes and another war began in Europe.

It became noticeable that this lightheartedness started fading on all fronts. Immediately, the questions came up: How does a whole profession move forward without staring paralyzed at the news and consequences of the various threats approaching? How fast and especially in what way can we react to these circumstances as architects for some betterment?

Since the profession is torn between being service-based on the one hand and claiming responsibility and willingness to impact society positively on the other, the effort will have to be divided among all players involved in the building industry, including financiers, policymakers, and governments. The requirements are so diverse, complex, and sometimes contradicting, that it will be necessary that all parties get together, communicate and argue various positions to achieve sustainable and worthy results. Just as stated in the article "Can Architecture Solve Our Crises?" by Ben Willis: *The leverage of a developer, planner, or politician may be different than that of an architect, but if they have a silver-bullet solution to these crises, they're holding out on us. The rather obvious truth is that solutions to big problems require "ecosystems of solutions," and the "ecosystem of solutions" to problems plaguing the built environment is made up of planning, financing, designing, constructing, and inhabiting.*[1]

However, what to plan, finance, design, and construct to make a difference, with all participants working synergistically, is up for debate. The very urgently needed new ideas about how we live, work, and therefore build, will be less likely to be provided by developers, clients or politicians, and governments alone. Architecture attracts a lot of highly motivated, optimistic, and skilled people that have the power to invent for betterment. These skill sets are nurtured within academic training and later considered valuable for professional practice for open calls and idea competitions. Unfortunately, many architects are forced to concentrate on the purely service-based side of architecture due to the economic necessities and timeframe of the practicing profession later in their careers. Therefore, architecture is often viewed as the solemn beautifier, homebuilder, and square-foot maximizer for developers or other clients, and a significant gap exists between society's idea of architecture and the profession itself.[2]

Luckily several technological advancements developed that can help the industry to become an active and efficient agent in developing strategies for a hopefully more sustainable way of planning and construction. Artificial Intelligence, mass customization, 3D printing, cloud computing, and various digital simulation and planning applications are helping in altering and modifying specific architectural visions on multiple scales. Thanks to that radical shift in digital production, buildings and cities can produce more energy than they need, can be constructed more sustainably and material efficiently, and adapt more quickly to changing circumstances. With these tools available to the profession lies a lot of potential to develop and produce the cities for the future we are hoping to live in one day.

As an architecture studio within an academic setting, we have the possibility and privilege to detect, address and develop schemes that could positively impact the long run. We are probably not the task force to provide immediate relief when a crisis hits, but we could keep on focusing on working on bold strategies and statements that could lead to improvements in the future. To address the large variety of problems we are facing and head into, we will need people that can focus, reinvent, walk lesser-known paths and challenge the current status quo. People that thrive working in teams, are able to argue and are persistent in advocating sustainable ideas, and are curious and critical about technological and digital progress. Architects can provide some of the above, and we should be confident that these skills will be of use if we communicate them well, be aware of current developments and be resilient to keep the strength to do the job.

However, what to plan, finance, design, and construct to make a difference, with all participants working synergistically, is up for debate. The very urgently needed new ideas about how we live, work, and therefore build, will be less likely to be provided by developers, clients or politicians, and governments alone. Architecture attracts a lot of highly motivated, optimistic, and skilled people that have the power to invent for betterment.

1   Ben Willis, "Can Architecture Solve Our Crises?," ArchDaily, (March 14, 2020), www.archdaily.com/935492/can-architecture-solve-our-crises.

2   Ned Cramer, "Architecture Is an Antidote," The Journal of the American Institute of Architects, (July 12, 2017), www.architectmagazine.com/design/editorial/architecture-is-an-antidote_o?utm_medium=website&utm_source=archdaily.com.

05

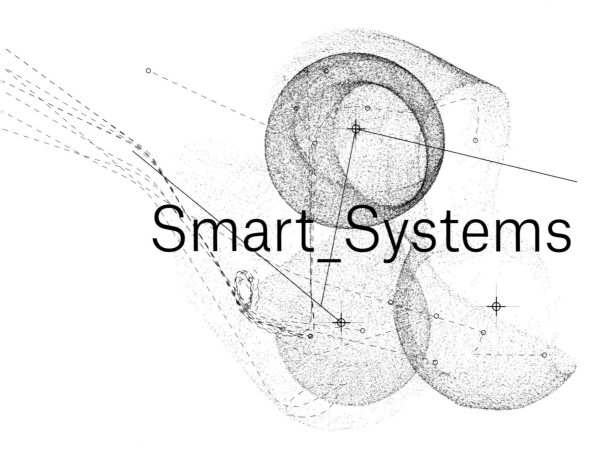

Smart_Systems

A critical aspect of "architectural intelligence" must emphasize socio-cultural transformation. Cities are testbeds where environmental and health inequality, rampant globalization and commercialization, aspects of control and censorship, and political instability all play a role in putting a city's vitality, and quality of civic life, in jeopardy. Architects working synergistically with urban planners and other critical stakeholders—politicians, policymakers, citizen groups—will inevitably need to shift strategies toward a focus on repair and welfare, community empowerment, democratic processes, and resilient urban developments. These actions require expertise and accessibility to knowledge systems and information. Innovative practices presuppose an understanding of cultural legacies, collective visions, and the mastering of conceptual tools that indicate tendencies, needs, and collective aspirations. Technology has the power to enhance these efforts; however, a new model of citizenship can provide and safeguard an optimistic fate for urbanity. Inclusive governance that sets health and environmental equity and justice in the foreground will require new architectural platforms and a shape-shifting urban scenery. For diverse communities and identities to come forward as equally significant actors in the city fabric, new ways of documenting history, collective memory, and experience are necessary. This premise opens opportunities for developing new stances and novel forms of cultural practices, including art institutions, trade networks, working and living environments and, most importantly, open, accessible, and engaging educational structures.

The projects featured in this chapter, under the title "Smart_Systems," emphasize the value of adaptable urban systems and programming, the interrelation of artificial and biological intelligence, the virtual counterparts of physical space, and their integration into a new and vital contemporary architecture.

Concepts such as resource efficiency, bottom-up planning, circular economy, new governance and city management forms, and public participation have driven the design endeavors. Industrial robots, automated fabrication apparatuses, and machine learning processes meet city-planning strategies and innovative urban typologies

to design new city forms. These include information and historical archives, buildings of knowledge and memory, art institutions and virtual platforms of civic expression, research facilities, and venues for making knowledge and research accessible to a broader public. Their shared endeavor is to articulate the architectural possibilities of the years ahead and the collaborative visions that will define how cities will transform in the following decades of our century.

BORDERS OF PLURALITY
A New Urban Morphogenesis

⊗ VIENNA, AUSTRIA

"Borders of Plurality" is an attempt to decipher the increasingly complex nature of urban spaces. The project aims to reinterpret existing urban frameworks without making a tabula rasa; rather, it uses the combinatorial potential of artificial and biological intelligence to call for a new urban morphogenesis. The project is located in the Volkertviertel on the edge of Vienna's Augarten, where it serves as a testing ground for the potential of machine-learning-based tools and their applicability in the existing urban context.

Tilman Fabini, Lisa Marie Gerdes, Oliver Hamedinger, Raffael Stegfellner

BORDERS OF PLURALITY

Vienna has a long history of suppressing nature. The over-domestication of the Danube has made the cityscape what it is today. On a terraforming scale, traces of former floodplains and marshlands have been obliterated. Large-scale construction has sealed an exorbitant area and erased the biological actors outside the last remaining fenced fortresses; the so-called public park areas. Neoliberal policies have created an urban fabric that is increasingly homogeneous and rigid, ill-equipped to meet the challenges of tomorrow. Programs and typologies have been deliberately separated, and the public space in between has been increasingly controlled in the name of traffic, security, and surveillance. These urban typologies are not only socially unsustainable, but also incapable of providing radical solutions to changing environmental concerns and the reality of an impending climate crisis.

In the wake of drastic environmental impacts, cities must radically change to compensate for new climatic conditions and overcome unsustainable practices. As part of this evolution, rethinking the street is an essential component, and ecological change can be used to explore new compositions of public and private space.

Borders of Plurality is an exploration of the combinatorial potential of artificial and biological intelligence in the context of augmented design processes. This methodology ultimately aims to create a more dynamic and dense urban composition that rejects the inflexible attitudes of human settlements toward their natural world. The principle of ecocentrism is a fundamental departure from the highly controlled baroque gardens of Vienna to a much more interdependent relationship between human and non-human actors. The urban structures of the future must be able to dynamically shape the mutually beneficial coexistence of the Anthropocene's natural and artificial actors.

A speculative redesigning of the city cannot be done from scratch, but must use the existing architectural infrastructure as a basis for its development. Through a hybridization of human and machine intelligence, the act of creation can be expanded beyond humanistic instincts to a more open system. By integrating various machine-learning techniques, it becomes possible to unravel the increasingly complex nature of urban spaces. The methodology aims to pool a variety of contextual data streams to identify patterns and dynamically counteract problematic environmental phenomena by uncovering specific gaps that allow problematic, monocultural developments to be counteracted.

180   Smart_Systems

To achieve this synergy, a series of computer workflows are created that oscillate between human and synthetic interventions in the design process. Within this collaborative framework, various machine learning networks are employed. First, the pix2pix architecture is used to decipher the semantic features of Vienna's current urban typology. A key advantage of using artificial intelligence in this context is the ability to reduce the high dimensionality of the complex reality of urban structures to a more tangible representation. This generalization is then passed to a series of generative networks programmed to explore the depth of all design possibilities within the confines of the original semantic features. The potential of this approach lies in its visual indeterminacy. The familiar yet strange contradictions in the result create a sense of alienation that allows established structures to be viewed through a different lens. This shift can make a meaningful contribution to creating new and unexpected possibilities for urban composition.

"Borders of Plurality" is an attempt to decipher the increasingly complex nature of urban spaces. The project aims to reinterpret existing urban frameworks without making a tabula rasa; rather, it uses the combinatorial potential of artificial and biological intelligence to call for a new urban morphogenesis.

BORDERS OF PLURALITY

Smart_Systems

Map data: Google, Image Landsat / Copernicus © 2022

THE PERMANENTLY TEMPORARY
In the Age of Gravity Independent Architecture

⊗ VIENNA, AUSTRIA

The project "The Permanently Temporary: In the Age of Gravity Independent Architecture" investigates the future of urban environments by using Vienna as a case study. It proposes a new ephemeral infrastructure that, while providing climatically controlled temporary spaces, integrates with the existing urban fabric to increase its dynamism, adaptability and thus capacity.
The project shows the development of the proposed infrastructure in four different locations in Vienna: Linke Wienzeile, Margaretengürtel-Wienfluss, industrial rooftops on the outskirts of the city, and open fields.

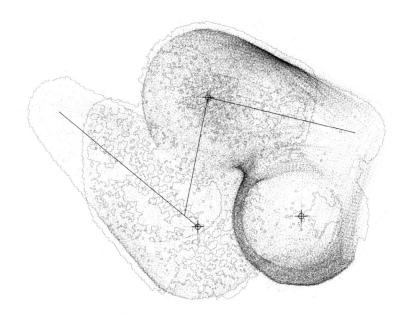

Viktória Sándor

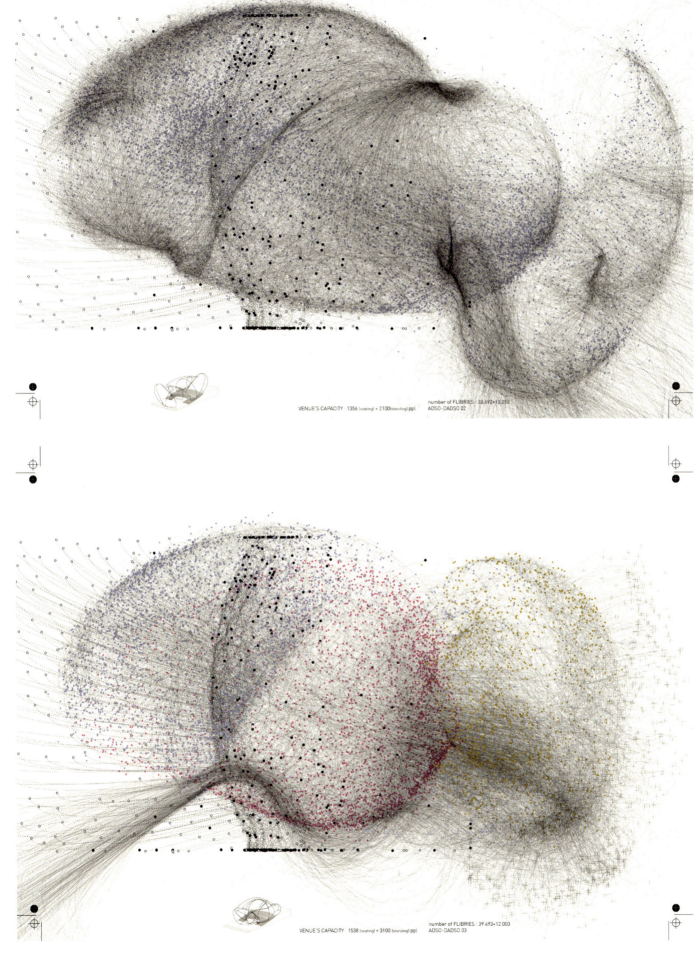

Re: Action

185

THE PERMANENTLY TEMPORARY

In urban environments, evolving issues caused by population growth, climate change, and changing patterns of social behavior, call for the exploration of new architectural and urban design strategies. The rigidity of the physical environment and the increasing value of the notions of temporality in everyday life are creating tension in the functioning of global cities. One way of resolving this tension is to increase the adaptability and responsiveness of physical space, with the focus on inner-urban environments.

The project proposes that temporary architecture has the potential to increase the adaptive capacity and responsiveness of the already built environment, and by turning itself into a new, spatially integrable urban infrastructure is able to respond to: urban population growth by densifying the city with the intensification of its urban volume; climate change by turning buildings and urban space into responsive, dynamically changing multifunctional systems; and changing patterns of social behavior by improving the fluidity of the physical space.

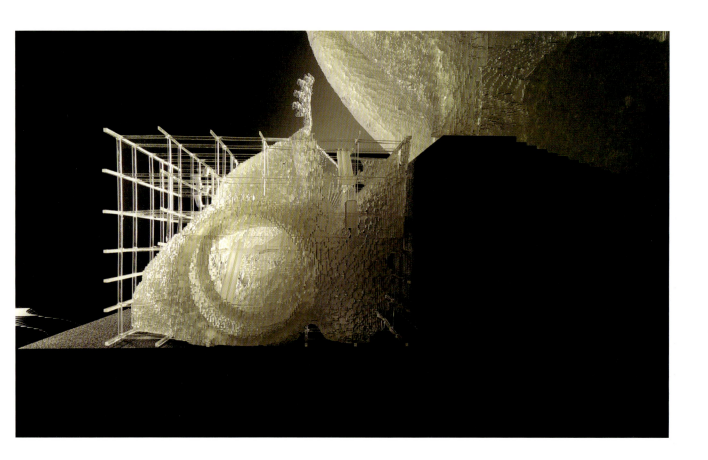

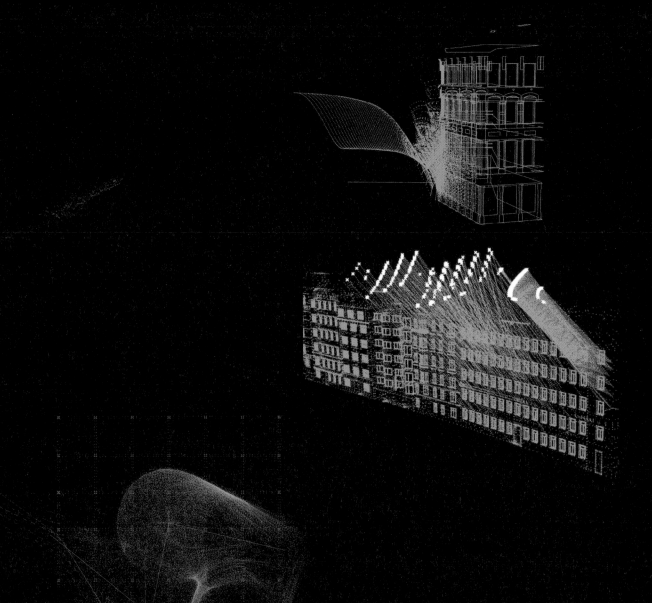

MAPPING THE URBAN FABRIC FOR QUALITY IMROVEMENT   DETECTING POTENTIAL SITES FOR TEMPORARY ARCHITECTURE TO APPEAR

LACK OF LIGHT   NOISE POLLUTION   SNOOZED STREETS   EMPTY PLATFORMS

Re: Action

187

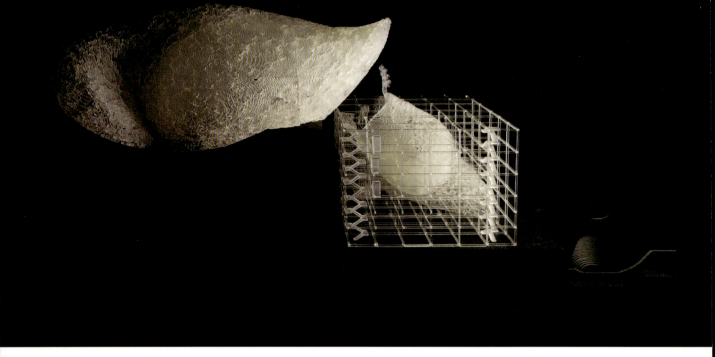
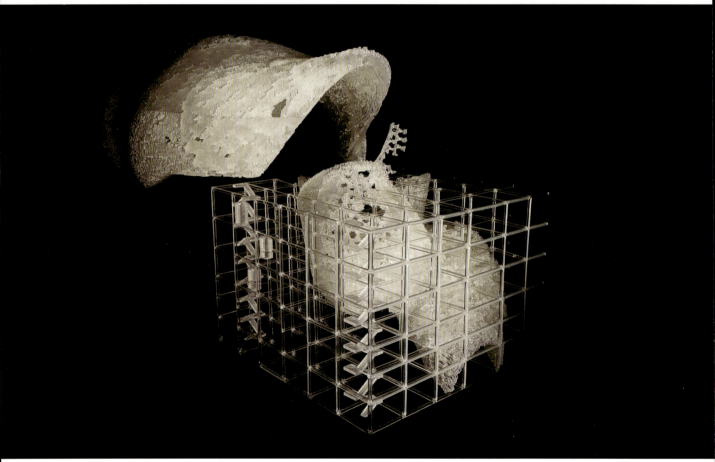

The project is developed on a multi-dimensional timeline that supports the evolutionary explorations of new, "permanently temporary" infrastructural interventions and their speculative impacts on urban dynamics. The timeline is divided into three main phases: Today, Tomorrow, and After Tomorrow. In the first phase, the project assumes that unmanned aerial vehicles will not only become supporters (builders) of the construction process, but also active building blocks of short-lived structures. This will reduce the time needed to build, transform, and demolish climate-controlled temporary spaces, leading to the design of the "drones of tomorrow." In the second phase, the project proposes a new design for the unmanned omnicopter (a research project by Raffaello D'Andrea, ETH Zurich) and calls it "FLIBRI" ("flying brick"). Flibries—the drones of tomorrow—can generate and store energy, radiate heat, provide and reflect light, and thus create a specific microclimate to provide optimal properties for new functions at locations that could not happen before. In phase three, the integration of the Flibri system into the urban volume is visualized in four evolutionary steps. The project's narrative emphasizes the changing relationship between the existing static urban fabric and the new Flibri system, while highlighting the changing purposes of the new infrastructure and its impact on urban dynamics.

With the proposed Flibri system, the project envisions a utopian future with sustainable urban growth and architecture. As a reaction to urban population growth, flibries increase the density of a given urban volume by temporarily isolating outdoor spaces. By recording the fluctuation frequencies of the used capacity in the interior and exterior volumes of the city, potential sites for temporary architecture are detected and populated with climatically controlled spaces on demand. The ideal sites for ephemeral functions include vacant land, residual urban spaces—and forgotten platforms such as roofs, terraces, and spatial niches that do not provide the necessary quality or are over-regulated for permanent design—as well as semi-used or unused snooze-zones, streets, and urban junctions, whose use-capacity can potentially be increased, but only at specific time intervals. The promise of the project is that the use of ephemeral architectural systems in cities can provide new responses to the changing value of space and bring about changes in the way we use our built environment.

If architecture could be ephemeral and adaptive, the existing city volume could be programmed more efficiently by the activation of its time-dependent snooze-zones. The resulting shift in the urban pattern would support the intensification of the city and establishment of a new social contract.

BREAKING THE 4TH WALL
A New Parliament

⊗ VIENNA, AUSTRIA

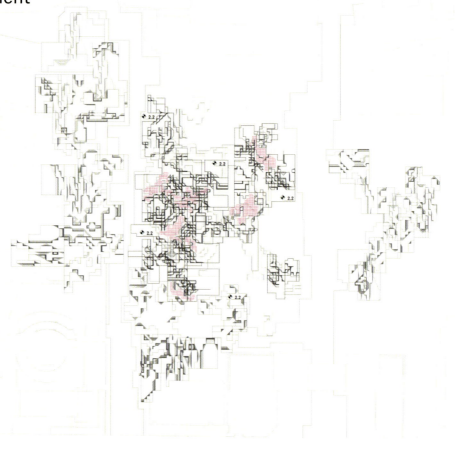

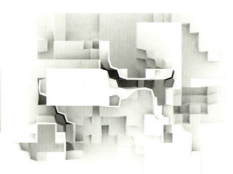

Mathias Juul Frost, Silvia Nanu, Andrej Strieženec

190   Smart_Systems

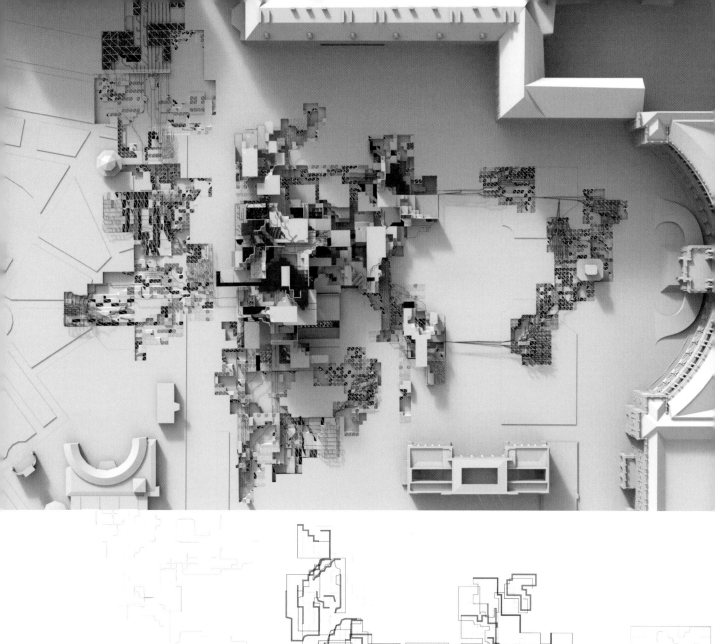
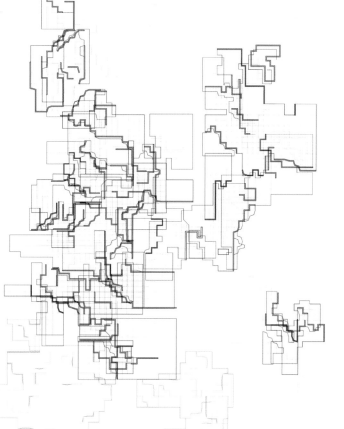

Re: Action

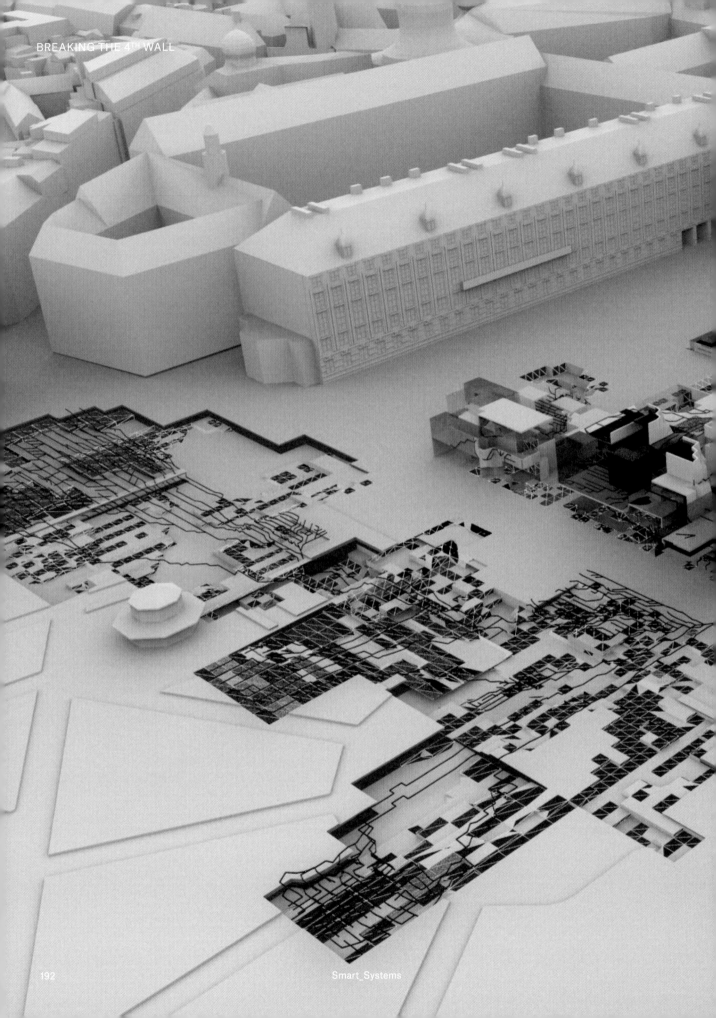

Re: Action

TOKYO 2121 MEGASTRUCTURE
Urban Industry in the Age of Artificial Intelligence

⊗ TOKYO, JAPAN

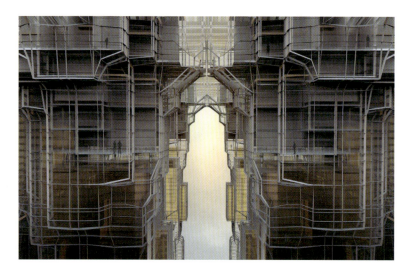

Alex Ahmad, Ludmila Janigova, Gakku Jumaniyasova, Silvia Nanu

194   Smart_Systems

TOKYO 2121 MEGASTRUCTURE

Re: Action

[$$$]_ART
An (Id)entity Totem

⊗ LOS ANGELES, USA

Dennis Schiaroli

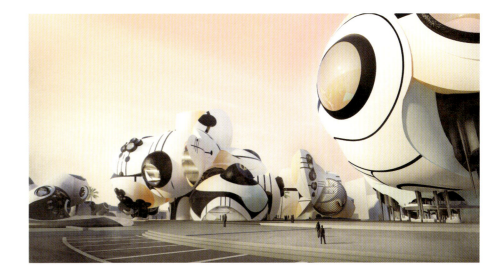

Re: Action

06

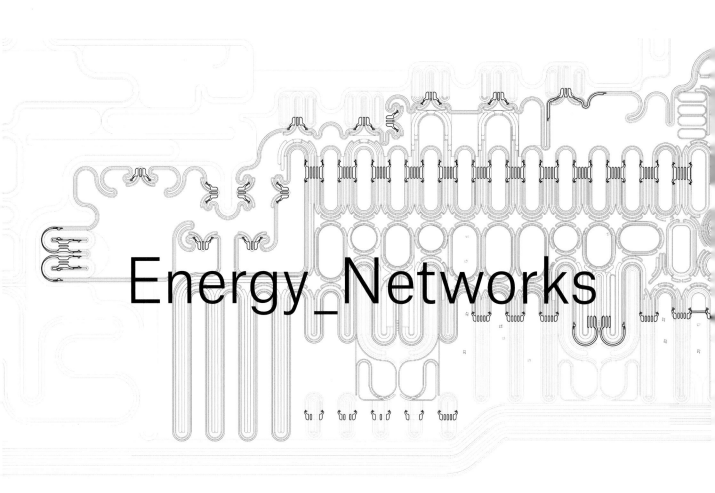

Energy_Networks

It is apparent today that to help societies reach pre-industrial global warming levels, and thus reverse the human-induced environmental catastrophe of the planet, the phasing out of the fossil fuel industry and the global transition to sustainable forms of energy is a shared prerogative and yet a complex undertaking as addressing environmental concerns reveals interconnected, underlying aspects of societal and political structures and co-dependencies. The production of energy is related to all activities of our modern world. Agriculture, transportation, construction, and resource extraction all require consumption of large amounts of energy to keep the world in motion. The call to stop the limitless extraction and exploitation of earth's finite resources is a call to turn away from industrial methods of energy production and consumption and modes of carbon-fueled mobility. Breakthroughs in science, technology, and engineering based on power strategies operating solely with renewable energies and sustainable resources as their base, promise to revolutionize the future of mobility—with this, new opportunities for environmentally coherent architecture and city-planning strategies will emerge.

Energy_Networks is a collection of architectural proposals focusing primarily on climate-resilient and sustainable models for habitation and interconnectivity. The projects incorporate the potential of digital technologies and scientific discoveries that open pathways to some intriguing new possibilities for architecture. Mainly, these projects focus on a new architectural role in a post-industrial future, where specific programs and building types become outdated and give rise to novel and innovative forms of urban programming and planning.

On the following pages, some projects place an "energy" focused lens on building types such as airports and their potential for transformation from present-day mass transportation hubs to a new type of building infrastructure based on a pattern of sustainable growth in response to the ecological, economic, and sanitary issues that increasingly challenge cities.

Other architectural investigations include: a look at self-powered green hydrogen technologies and their potential impact on building form and materials, a project that utilizes renewable resources and recycled materials as the primary drivers for new types of urban structures, and another that embraces new fabrication techniques to support and defend the interconnection of sprawling urban settlements.

In all of these projects, there is a combined interest in designing viable commercial and economically sustainable approaches to the future of building design and urban planning.

TH⁹⁰R[IV]E
The First Neotechnic Power Plant

⊗ TIANJIN, CHINA

"The First Neotechnic Power Plant" is a fourth-generation nuclear power plant located at the port of Tianjin, China. The site was the center of one of the biggest industrial disasters in China's history, when in 2015, "an overheated container of dry nitrocellulose"[1] led to a devastating explosion of 800 tons of ammonium nitrate in a chemical factory.[2]

    The explosions of Tianjin are evidence of how devastating technological dissimulation can be. Tianjin's strategic geographical position, since it lies only a train ride away from the capital city, Beijing, and of course, its economic importance as the world's third biggest industrial port, have led the area to grow frantically within the last fifty years. In 1953, the municipality had 2.6 million inhabitants, and now it has almost 15 million. The rapidly urbanizing economy gladly accepted the lax enforcement, lack of transparency, and quick approvals that made China's rapid economic growth possible in the first place. The port, as well as a big part of Tianjin's industry, was once located outside the city. Over time, however, the city has grown around it. This also applies to the big coal power plants in the area, since, naturally, economic growth also needs a lot of energy. That is why the strategic placement of TH⁹⁰R[IV]E on this delicate site is highly important.

Luca Melchiori

Energy_Networks

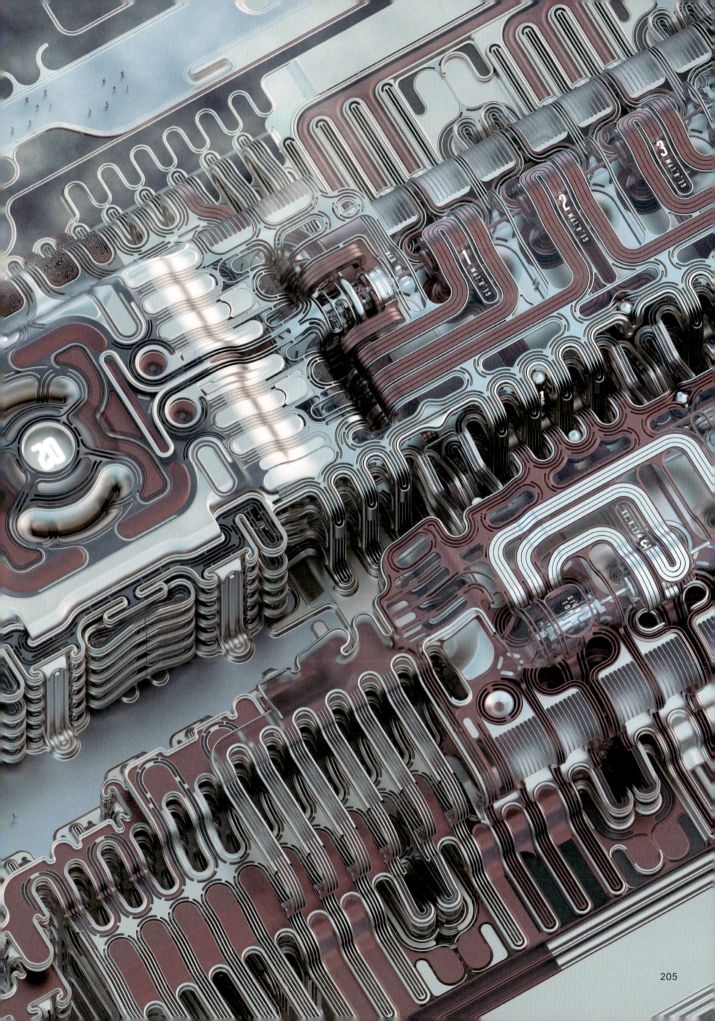

TH⁹⁰R[IV]E

The aim of TH⁹⁰R[IV]E is to unfold the most advanced and secure technologies of energy production and demonstrate the overcoming of the paleotechnic bonds and pseudomorphic contradictions of the present age, which have been thoroughly described by Lewis Mumford in his *Technics and Civilization*. By facilitating the commitment of many countries, it shifts the focus on current scientific challenges and intensifies the voice of science all over the world. It should serve as a catalyst for the expansion of the scientific language and illustrate the importance of technology in uniting countries, and therefore be advantageous to the whole of mankind. By creating a space that personifies these neotechnic values, it should help in preserving the present quality of life for centuries. It celebrates human ingenuity, spirituality, sensuality, and its deepest connection to nature.

According to Mumford, we are convinced that we are in the full bloom of the neotechnic period, but still, we choose to increase mechanical performance over environmental equilibrium. Forests are still being cut, minerals carelessly mined or pumped out of the ground, and radioactive waste either buried underground or dumped into the ocean. As shown in Tianjin, the miscarriage of technology treats not only the environment with extreme cruelty but also humanity. The accuracy that technology and science embodies seems to be demolishing the beauty and elegance of nature. That is why technology is often seen as a malicious element, heedless of human life. In our society, life often gets judged by the extent to which it ministered to progress, but progress not by the extent to which it ministers to life.[3] People died in the coal pit or cotton mill during the industrial revolution; now they suffocate in Xingtai, Boading, or Tianjin. Technological gains do not get automatically assimilated into society. They need equally important adaptations in politics.

By creating a space that personifies these neotechnic values, it should help in preserving the present quality of life for centuries. It celebrates human ingenuity, spirituality, sensuality, and its deepest connection to nature.

Energy_Networks

Certainly, one of the most outstanding examples of technological misappropriation is the derailing of nuclear technology due to bellicose and pecuniary influences. All the current nuclear reactors there are today are based on either the Breeder Reactor (BWR – 20%) or the Light Water Reactor (PWR – 69%), developed post-WW2 from the atomic bomb. We could have had a completely different world if we had chosen a different path during the Cold War, when experiments like "ARE" or the Molten Salt Reactor Experiment, which, with their completely different fuel cycle in comparison to conventional reactor design, proved to have a huge potential for clean and sustainable energy. Additionally, as Thorium could serve as the primary fuel within a molten salt reactor, it would free our society from the deadly bonds of the mine, since being a byproduct of coal mines, there is so much Thorium already in stock that it could fuel our energy demand for over one thousand years.

TH⁹⁰R[IV]E

The architectural aim of TH⁹⁰R[IV]E is to be a mediator between the public and science by creating a space where the architecture is defined by the machine but created for the human. The turbine islands of the power plant should be the primary interface where these two entities meet. They constitute the extension of the green park, where once the explosions of Tianjin happened. The openness of the space should blur the border between the inside and the outside of the turbine island. The translation of the machine into architectural elements like a roof, column, or slab, allows the creation of a space in which the machine doesn't inhabit the space, but defines its spatiality. With this potential of engaging with the public in almost an instructional way, the architecture of TH⁹⁰R[IV]E should help raise awareness of nuclear technology's potential and clear the haze of misconception that surrounds it.

    The world desperately needs the neotechnic virtues embodied within molten salt reactors. Besides being the first power plant representing these values, it helps to disperse the haze of prejudice enveloping nuclear energy by spreading the scientific language and word of peace.

1   Wikipedia contributors, "2015 Tianjin explosions," Wikipedia, The Free Encyclopedia, accessed December 22, 2022, https://en.wikipedia.org/w/index.php?title=2015_Tianjin_explosions&oldid=1126878631.
2   Wikipedia, The Free Encyclopedia, "2015 Tianjin explosions."
3   Lewis Mumford, *Technics and Civilization* [1934], Reprint ed. (University of Chicago Press, 2010), pp. 167–173.

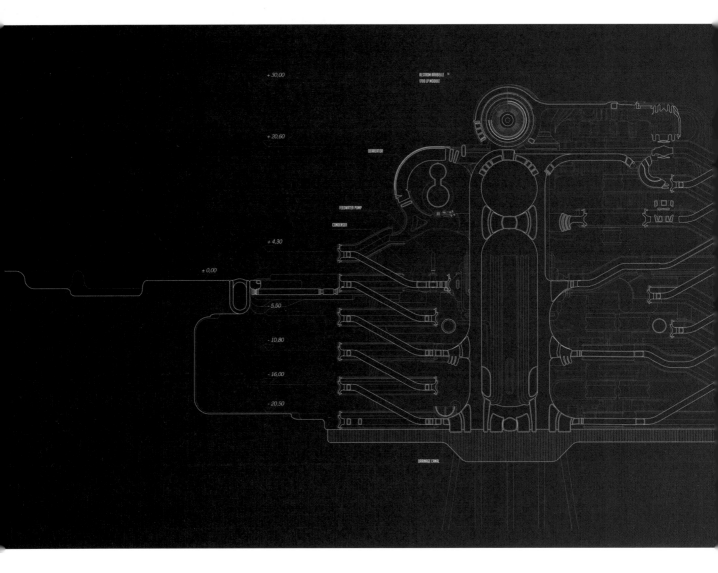

The world desperately needs the neotechnic virtues embodied within molten salt reactors. Besides being the first power plant representing these values, it helps to disperse the haze of prejudice enveloping nuclear energy by spreading the scientific language and word of peace.

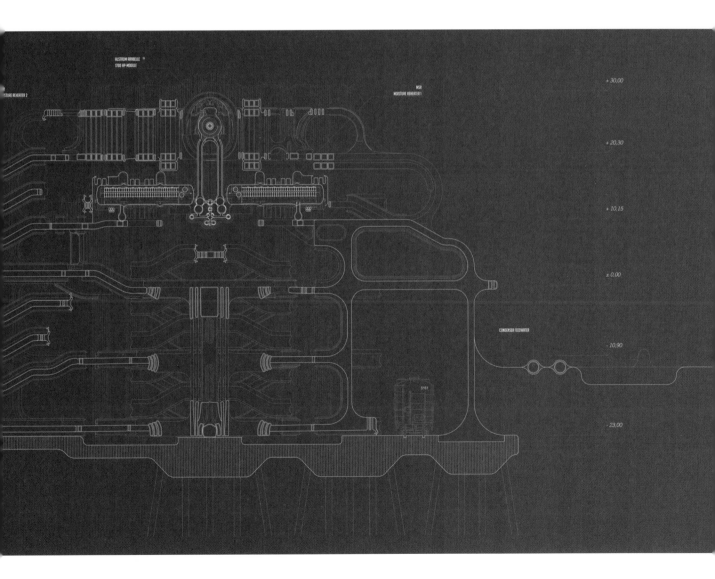

METAir
Vertical Air Transportation System

⊗ PARIS, FRANCE

"METAir" stands for a new vertical mobility system of transportation. Vertical mobility represents the new era of transportation for humankind. To prove the idea, we studied the current condition of Charles de Gaulle Airport (CDG). Moreover, we propose to extend the project beyond the boundaries of the airport site—to the streets of Paris itself. Therefore we came up with two different, but related, scales for the project: "AIRSTATION," which operates as urban mobility within Paris and "AIRNODE," the substantial modernization of CDG.

Kyryll Dmytrenko, Zhiyi Zhang

Re: Action

METAir

To integrate AIRSTATION into the city fabric, we needed a compact and elegant solution with no compromise on function. Seeking these qualities, we referred to the natural ability of pinecones to decrease in size. We found parallels in their functions: pinecones keep their seeds for a proper moment to disperse them, and Vertiport keeps its drones until the user calls them. So, when the drone is needed the structure opens; otherwise, it stays closed and the visual mass of the structure is reduced as much as possible.

The crucial point of our project is to address the rising issue of air quality in Paris: embedded air-capture devices that replace certain units on a tower are dedicated to CO_2 and NO_2 capture. This system is powered by another type of unit that transforms wind flows to produce energy by displacing electrodes. The amount of energy produced would be sufficient to charge the drones and supply the air capture devices. In such a way, the METAir mobility system not only produces a zero-carbon footprint but also purifies the air from the emissions left from previous decades of dominating fossil fuels.

Studying the master plan of CDG Airport, we found that around 32.4 km² of land is occupied by only four runways. Everything else is either storage or other airplane maintenance facilities. Such an inefficient layout causes significant delays in moving aircraft, waiting to land or take off, around the master plan. But what if we could optimize it by using a substantially smaller piece of land? And why do we need to constantly move the aircraft from one place to another?

We came up with a drone system—a system of rotatable platforms capable of interchanging and maintaining drones. Glass and carbon fibers are main materials for this system. These materials show very good structural properties and lightness. Moreover, from the architectural side, small gaps between the fibers help reduce the visual "solidity" of the structure.

Distributed around the city, following our vision, the METAir mobility system will significantly change the city and people's lives. Greenery will replace roads and other places currently occupied by on-ground vehicles and the streets will eventually be reclaimed by people. This new type of air transportation will breathe a new dose of oxygen into the city and human lives.

Collage with photo by Alexander Kagan on Unsplash

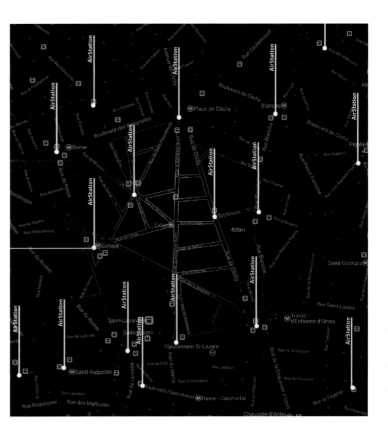

Map data: Google © 2022

METAir

Greenery will replace roads and other places currently occupied by on-ground vehicles and the streets will eventually be reclaimed by people.

Re: Action

YGGDRASIL
The Future of Urban Connectivity

⊗ HEATHROW, UK

"Yggdrasil: The Future of Urban Connectivity" is located at Heathrow Airport in the United Kingdom. Just like the Yggdrasil tree, our project aims to become a tool for organizing and bringing together different worlds at the same time, a critique and reaction to the obsoletion of airport typology as we currently know it. It is well-known that emissions have been growing steadily during the last decades and, looking at the relationship between the City of London and Heathrow in particular, scoring comparable values in terms of CO_2 footprint.

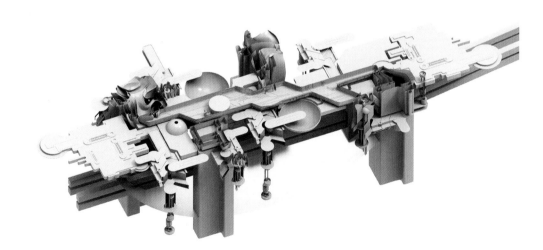

Witchaya Jingjit, Anastasia Smirnova, Simonas Sutkus, Patricia Tibu

Energy_Networks

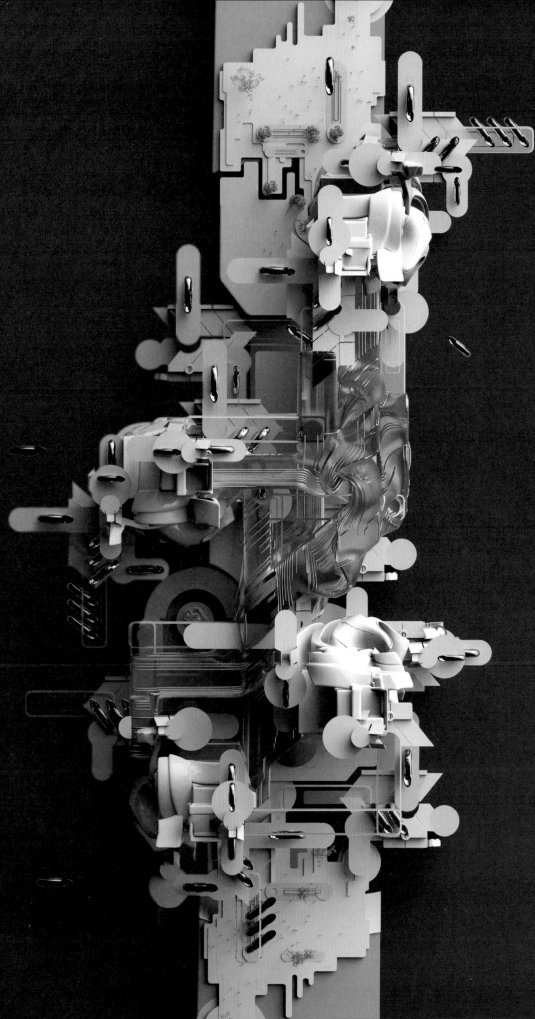

YGGDRASIL

Establishing an enclosed CO_2 cycle within the airport was one of our main drivers. Therefore, each tower cluster fulfills CO_2 synthesizing functions where the gas is turned into either energy, fuel for the planes, or sediments that can then be used as building materials.

We created a vertical gate prototype that intends to act almost like a funnel for the CO_2 cycle, synthesizing it into products that achieve productivity such as energy, fuels, or even construction materials in buildings. As the main project premise is to capture CO_2 with wind flow geometry, the passenger circulation system was also based on aerodynamics.

In terms of functional organization, the design process is informed by our other two design drivers: obtaining a switching mechanism between long-distance and local air travel and enforcing the metropolitan character of the future airport. The upper part of the towers is designated for aircraft usage while the lower floors accommodate passenger-related functions. The core of the tower works as a carbon processing farm that then distributes the by-products within the rest of the project. The towers have a dominant machinist character, the airport platforms are highly flexible and also account for the management of the standby aircraft.

Although we tried to distinguish and separate between the different functions—agriculture, CO_2 sequestration, air travel, etc.—we tried to achieve visual connections that bring the space together in terms of human experience.

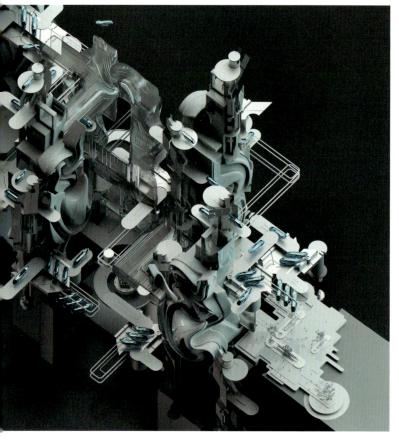

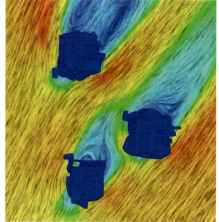

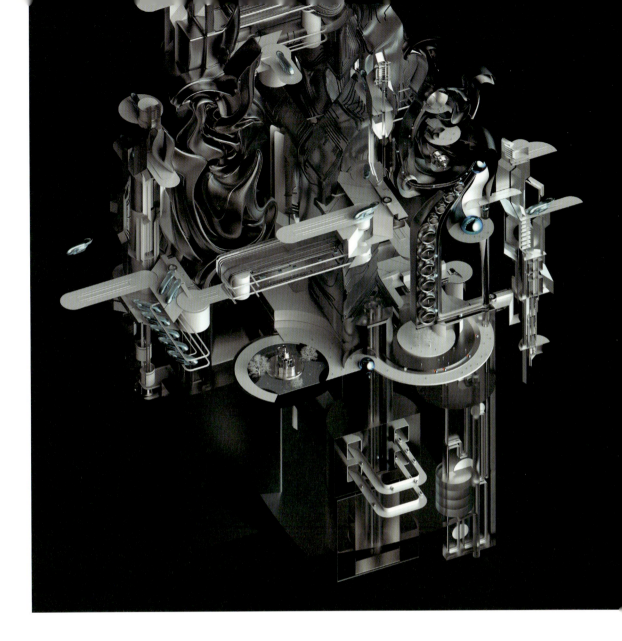

We used the plan to investigate the relationship between the tower's placement and the central passenger space. The passenger flow system emerges from this relationship and is especially geared towards achieving seamless switching between international and local air travel. The circulation and spatial distribution of the central space are also greatly influenced by the user experience. We are trying to achieve a meaningful space that would also have the capacity to exist outside the realm of the air travel industry.

The overall ambition for the central space was to achieve an atmosphere that facilitates the metamorphosing of the airport typology into a new programmatic logic that is less of a human processing machine and more of a plausible functional part of an urban scheme. With regards to the automation of the airport processes, they are mainly organized around a conveyor-belt strategy and are layered upon each other, some of them being exposed to the users. Therefore, while the system is automated, there is still a realization of the dynamic processes that inform an airport experience.

YGGDRASIL

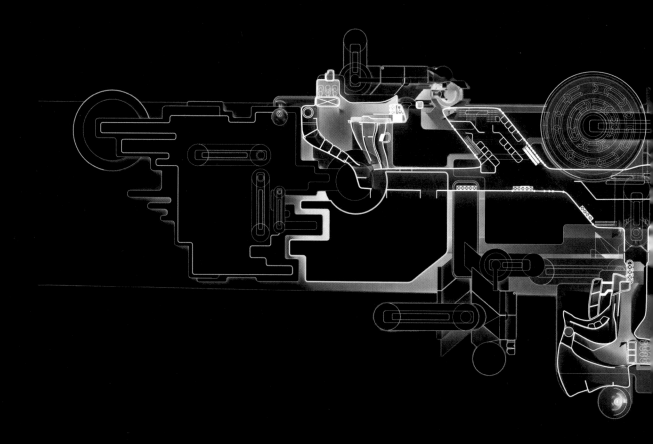

At ground level, there is a dense cross-laminar flow between the different means of transportation and the different user categories. This slowly dissipates in the higher levels since the building is distributing and guiding the different user categories.

Within the towers, the gates are disposed of in a vertically shifted fashion for the passenger flow to be optimized and the spatial usage to be maximized.

The project has ambitions to become a gate figure for the city; a threshold element that is informed by far more than just the functional aspects of air travel. Achieving an enclosed energy cycle and offering the possibility for human-oriented spaces that are meaningful in the larger urban scheme are important factors that have geared the project towards its current status.

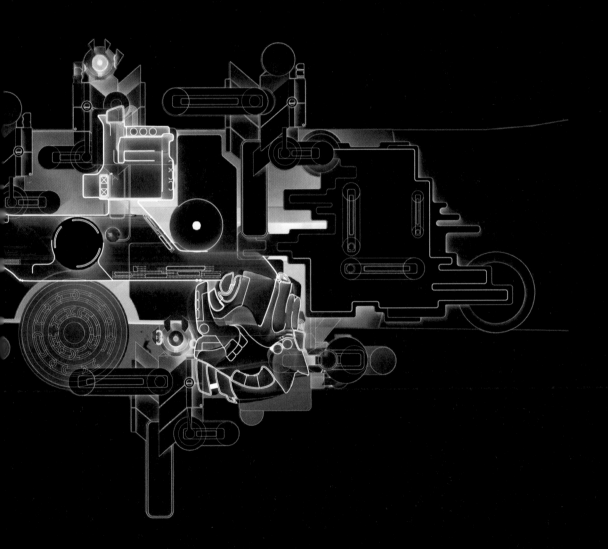

DIS(ASSEMBLE)
E-Mobility Futures

⊗ ROUTE 50, USA

Leonie Eitzenberger, Kieran Tait

222　　　　　　　　　　　Energy_Networks

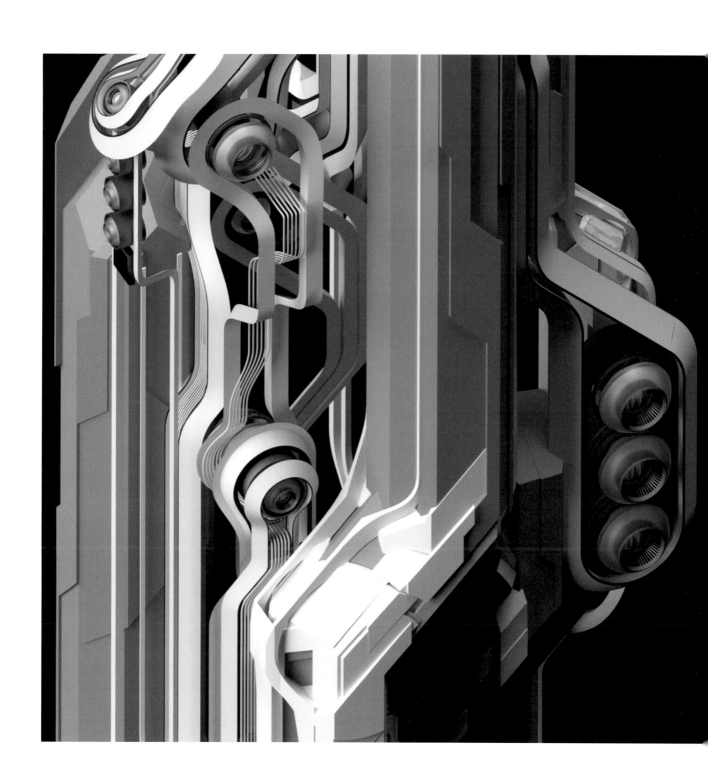

DIS(ASSEMBLE)

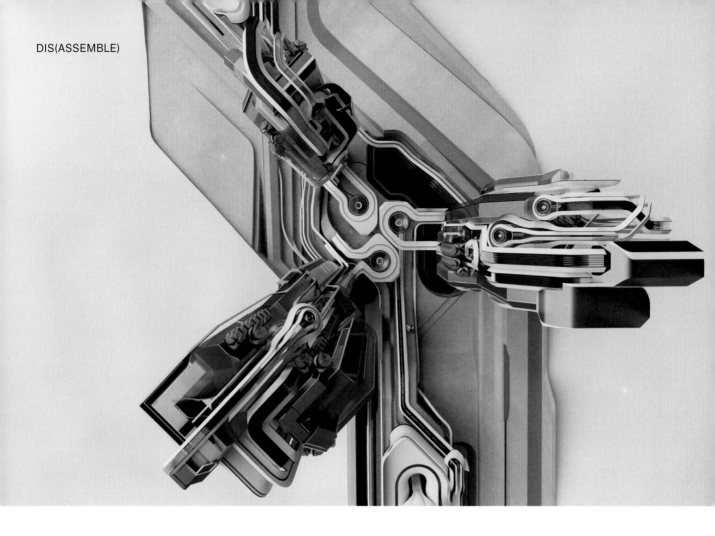

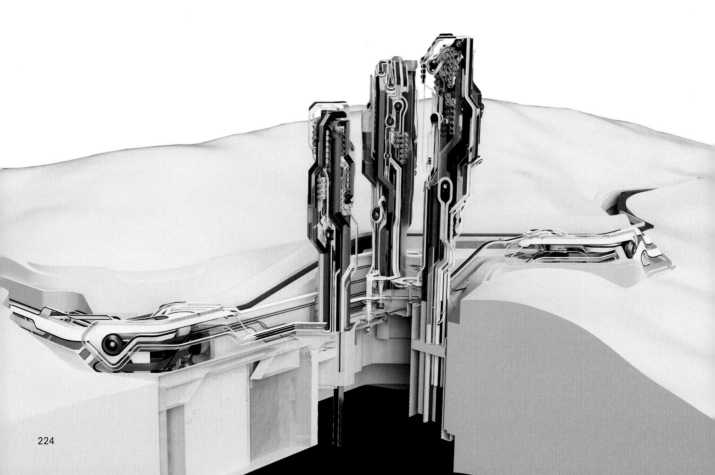

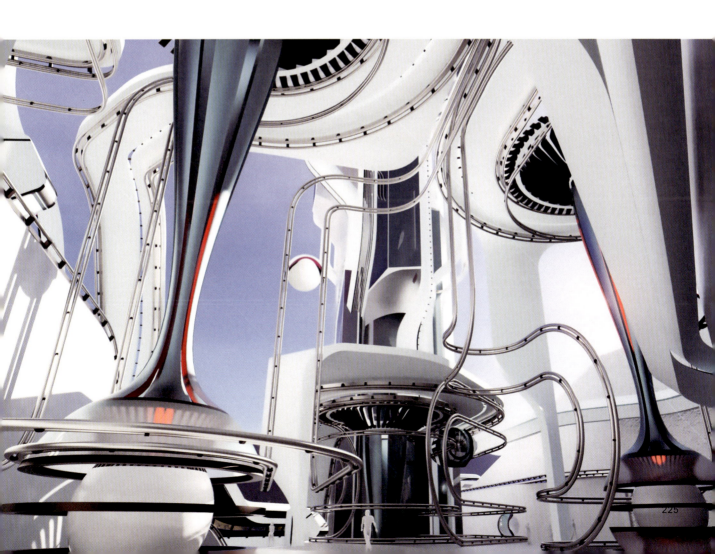

HYPER_MOBILITY
Accelerated Future Transportation Network

⊗ LOS ANGELES, USA

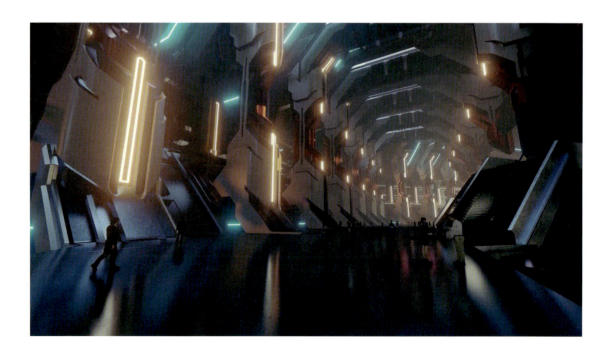

Kieran Tait

226 Energy_Networks

Re: Action

HYPER_MOBILITY

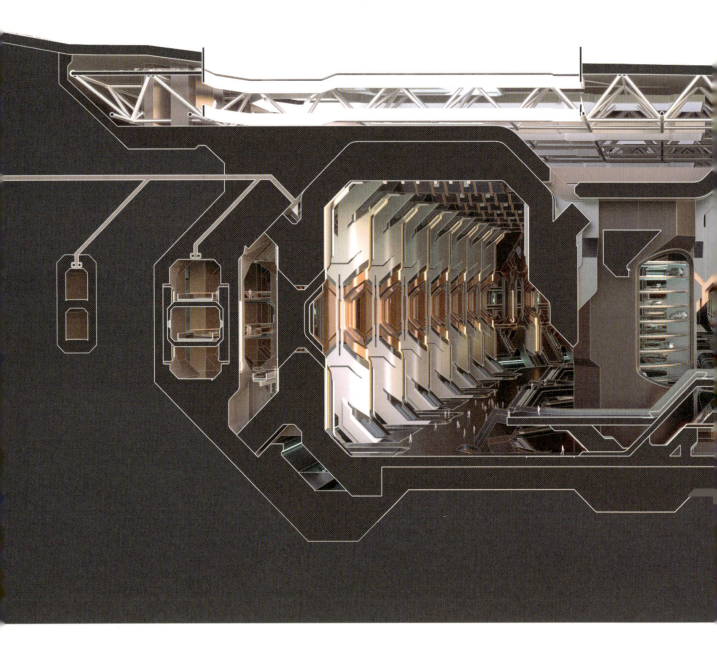

228　　　　　　　　　　　　　　　Energy_Networks

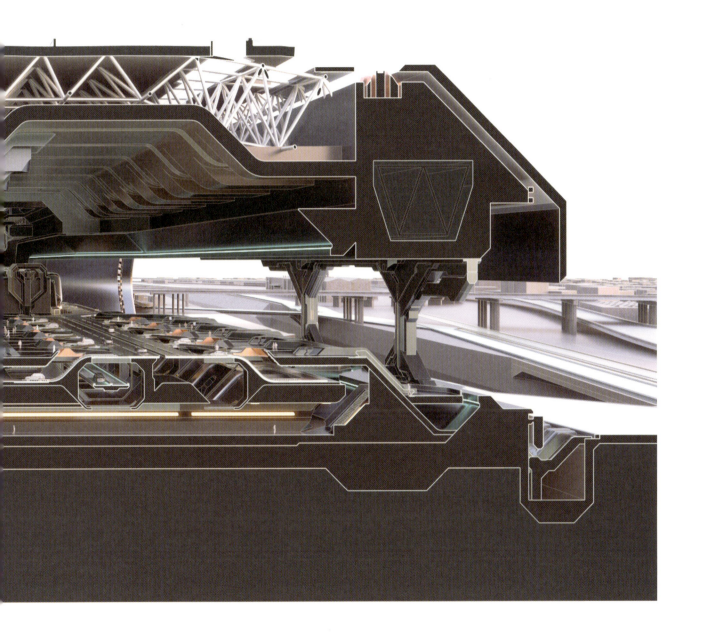

07

Transactive_Landscapes

The COVID-19 pandemic and today's unprecedented "climate shock" are but two of several phenomena impacting many aspects of our lives and cities. Today an urgent need for a renewed and revised focus on hygiene, health and wellbeing, and resiliency will be necessary for the future growth of cities.

In the coming years, radical urban-planning approaches, coupled with provocative architectural innovations, could lead the way to answering and affecting the complex global challenges that lie ahead. In this sense, architectural practices and building regulations must align with global situations, including responses to issues of mass migration on the one hand and tackling more mundane, yet equally critical, issues such as maintaining suitable air quality on the other. Today, for example, there is an increased interest in remote work, virtual meetings, and a collective global digital interconnectivity. Nevertheless, this technological integration has become socially problematic and impacted not only worklife dynamics but also education and all aspects of socialization. In this context, creativity and innovation are yielding an ever-increasing array of new approaches to all aspects of civic life. Social communication, healthcare, and hygiene in the built environment have become imperative for a city's sustainable future. From issues of mental and physical health equity to the welfare and accommodation of an aging population, from responses to pandemic outbreaks to the strengthening of environmental resilience—these are the critical vectors forming our thinking and strategies for the future of cities and their architecture.

Transactive_Landscapes is a collection of projects that embrace the dynamism and chaotic underpinnings of the ever-changing cityscape. These projects aim to discover new embodiments for the future of the built environment. Primarily tasked to work on operational and health-oriented urban structures, these projects suggest, instead, more positive ways for societies to provide for their citizenry. Here the measure of success is measured by social inclusion, dignity, and a renewed public attentiveness tied to healthy co-existence. These projects deal with the future of what one could call a "health culture" where medical facilities benefit the public good while ecological restoration provides for spaces of recuperation and repair. Architecture's "therapeutic potential" is at the center of this research, made apparent by various systems of transformation and activation of public realms and spaces, care for their citizenry, measuring success by values of social inclusion, democracy, and dignity, and public attention tied to a healthy co-existence with all lifeforms. These projects deal with the future of health culture and medical facilities, the benefits of recreational city programs for the public good, and the ecological restoration of radioactive and polluted territories within cities.

MIA
Medically Induced Apotheosis

⊗ GENEVA, SWITZERLAND

"MIA | Medically Induced Apotheosis" is an architectural proposal for a future pharma and health infrastructure. It hypothesizes the importance of habitual health and how it can be induced and encouraged through spatial design, location, and rethinking the current medical pipeline. It does this through a centralized system where medicinal plants are grown to demand for their surrounding communities whilst also accommodating space for pharmacognosy.

Jade Bailey, Emma Sanson

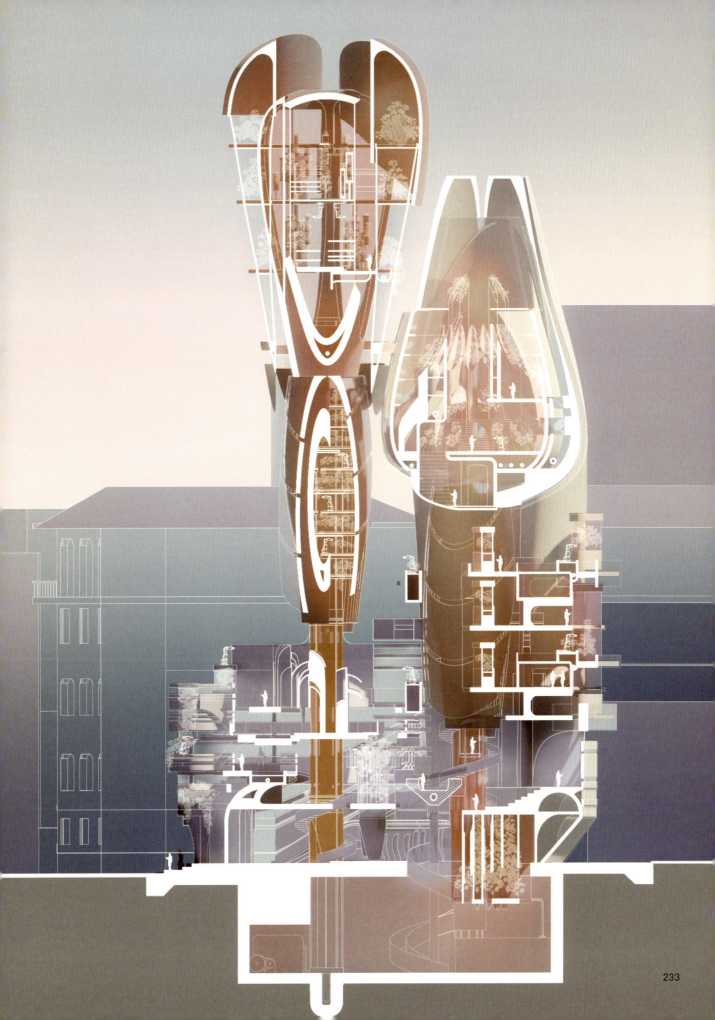
233

MIA In a world where climate change and increased risk of highly contagious pandemics have the probability of eradicating large percentages of our population, we are starting to focus on our health and wellbeing more than ever. The 21st-century definition of "health" encompasses everything from holistic and herbal approaches to self-awareness, healthy habits and routines, all the way to medicines and transhuman natures. Currently, the healthcare system suffers from a lot of inefficiencies that have enabled it to fall behind in its architectural stature and importance, offering a very rigid, stagnant and outdated experience. There are a multitude of new technologies coming to fruition—ready to be consumed in the medical market today—pushing forward the next generation of healthcare, health architecture, and perspectives on health culture and its impact within society.

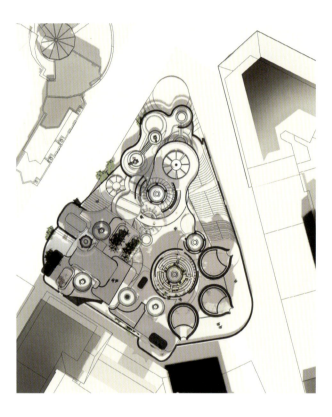

There are a multitude of new technologies coming to fruition—ready to be consumed in the medical market today—pushing forward the next generation of healthcare, health architecture, and perspectives on health culture and its impact within society.

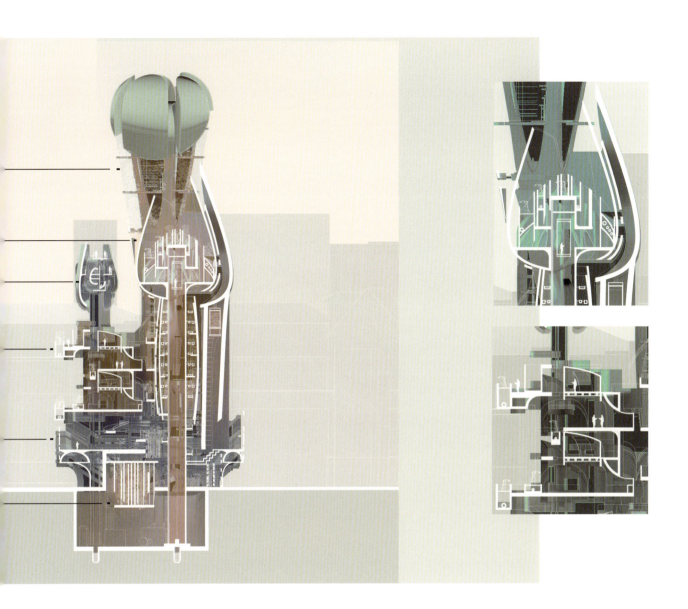

The design explores how these new scientific and technological feats can influence architecture and questions the extent to which it can play a role in preventing illness by encouraging habitual behavior toward personal health and wellbeing as a community and society. One of the design's main features in order to explore this is to provide transparency in the pharmaceutical industry and open up the process of medicinal research and production to allow a more personalized medication dosage and prescription. This makes testing more efficient and medicine more affordable and accessible, whilst localizing the pharmaceutical structure with the intent to reduce waste, streamline production, and increase energy efficiency within the process, from growth to consumption. This allows for the entire pharmaceutical procedure to be more trustworthy and dependable to coincide with a new age of health.

The design proposal is composed of a multitude of functions. The first and most prominent aspect of the design revolves around an open clinic, based in the heart of the city, for people to access daily. This is juxtaposed with a medicine cafe designed to exude transparency, and therefore openness, to both community and individual. The programs correlate to uniquely designed components that can be assembled in differing variations within a multitude of urban densities and structures. This allows the design to expand and retract depending on local needs and dependencies.
The gardens inside create pockets of solitude and respite from our often overwhelming and over-capitalistic urban realms. Public gardens are integrated and intertwined within the sealed research gardens, which entice visitors to the higher floors but also act as green lungs for the city.

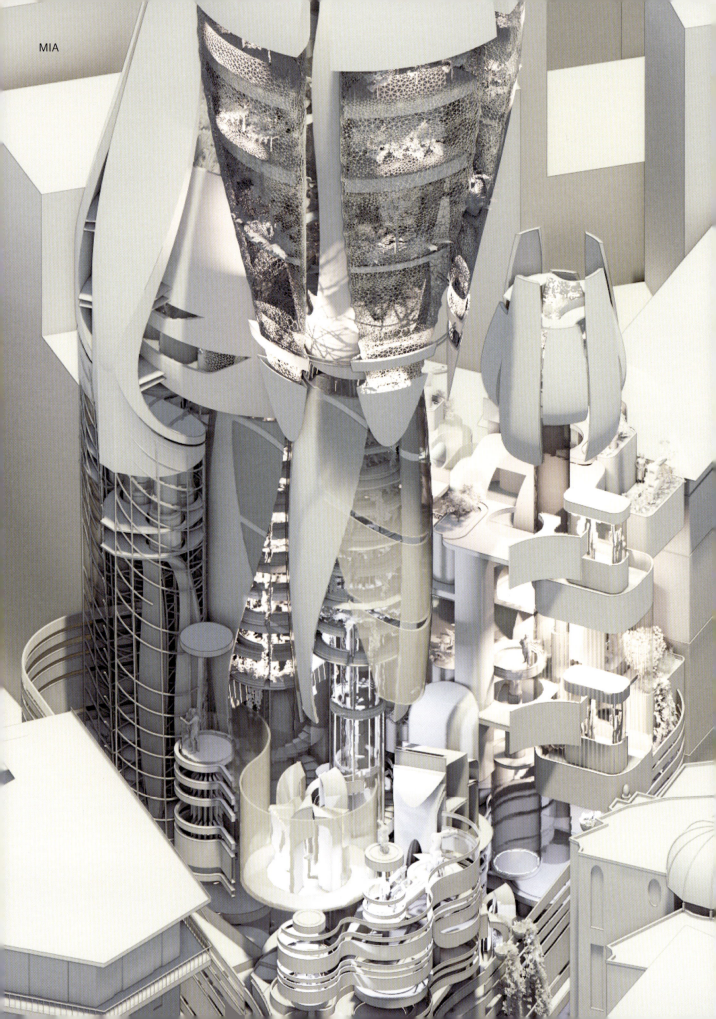

The internal spaces are designed to stimulate the brain and encourage user interaction by enhancing the natural, playful qualities of light, promoting natural and fluid space through which the body and mind can wander, fluctuating between open and cavernous spaces and cozy and intimate spaces in order to amplify physical awareness and provide varying degrees of social interaction between users. The different growth phases of the plants allow the internal space to morph with the seasons and local demand for medicines, designed with continual change in mind. Playing with the biophilic principles of prospect and refuge, the different areas and pavilions of the public space play on natural human tendencies to prefer observing without being observed —and having in very rudimentary terms "multiple escape routes." The circulation system revolves around the efficiency of workers and consists of a series of hydraulic lifts. By reducing the horizontal circulation system more space is created for research, testing and production. With the hydraulic elements changing the spatial appearance on an hourly basis, the conditions created are vibrant and continuously dynamic.

The proposal uses Geneva as a test ground to implement the scheme, as it is a pioneering city with regard to healthcare and therefore a prime location for developing a new strategy toward providing health. It aims to be a central hub of the community—where people attend daily, weekly, and monthly to gain access and replenish their medicines, vitamins, and minerals—offering integrated therapy tailored to each individual in spaces designed to de-stress and holistically enhance the effect of treatment. In doing so, it provokes a social, sustainable future surrounding healthcare that can be integrated and deployed into varying urban realms and densities.

Playing with the biophilic principles of prospect and refuge, the different areas and pavilions of the public space play on natural human tendencies to prefer observing without being observed— and having in very rudimentary terms "multiple escape routes."

VESTIGE
Academy of Sound

⊗ BERGEN, NORWAY

A decrease in biodiversity and loss of habitat are two major concerns that result from human intervention. While we have been slowly designing our environments, carving the continental crust to our heart's content and erecting elaborate dwellings that please the eye of the beholder, we have also been molding the dissonances of the invisible. Loud as a species, our sonic imprint has proliferated along with our expansion of territory. Muting others in our path, we are slowly leaving behind a monotonous noisescape where sounds for survival drown in the steady rhythm of our machines. Located in Bergen, Norway, "Vestige Academy of Sound" aims to visibly modify its surrounding sonic landscape, bringing to attention the power architecture holds over our audible environments.

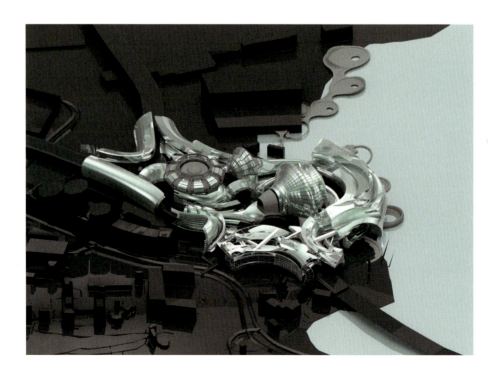

Emma Sanson

Transactive_Landscapes

VESTIGE

Eluded due to its intangible nature, the sonic environment of our cities has the potential to fill a major gap in how we design healthier cities if given a medium through architecture. Using spectrograms and noise maps, the project placement as well as its morphology come together to create a new approach to building with and for sound, and against noise. Exploring the divergent sonotones that appear at the intersection of nature and design, Vestige aims to become a new sonic category currently missing from conversations surrounding sound ecology. Balancing between the anthrophony and the geophony, the building creates a new hybrid soundscape named "archiphony."

Sound is connected to all elements of our physical domain. In the Academy of Sound, the users explore how their performance and learning can be affected by the spaces they use. Offering various rooms with a gradient of sizes and materials, the school encourages the students to explore how their performances and compositions can work together with the spaces.

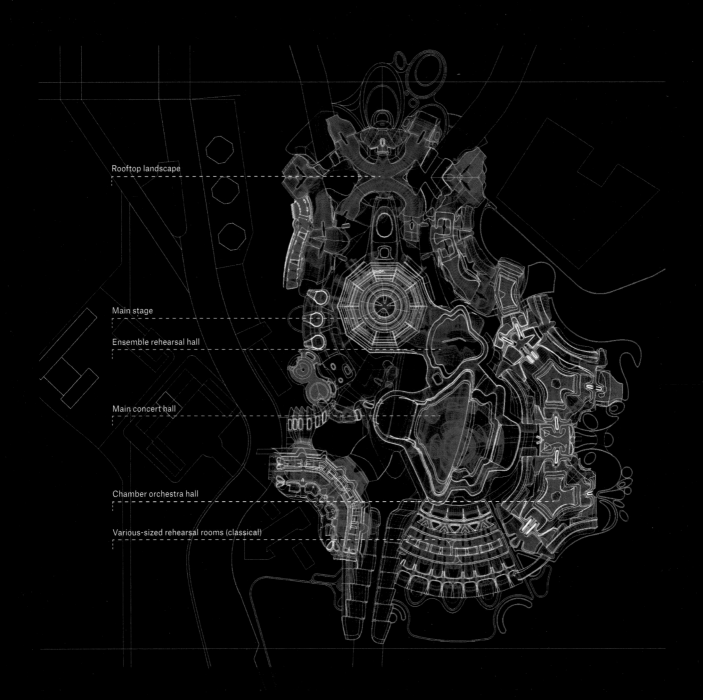

It becomes visible in research done by Krause that changes in landscapes where resident animals have evolved to use it from an auditory perspective can have fatal consequences whether it be marine, terrestrial, or freshwater ecosystems. Categorizing a new type of sonotope directly related to designed landscape can help put focus on the impact that sound has on our overall ecosystem and—in this wider context—the biodiversity of our planet. We have until now been shaping our societies on dichotomies. Audible, visible. Urban, rural. Natural, unnatural. Biotic, abiotic. The Archiphony, once established, will become a hybrid configuration, merging the biophony and geophony by human means into a new assembly. No longer building solely for humans, but for a complex amalgamation of inhabitants, the scales we see today will change dramatically, with the sonotopes of our cities no longer being as harmful as they are at present. The Archiphony, if explored, has the potential to bridge the gaps between the different disciplines that make up our urban environments, creating healthier conditions for its locals, as well as being a better neighbor for its surroundings.

Breaking with the tradition of spaces simply housing compositions of various natures, these new meandering configurations aim to inspire compositions to use the space as part of the piece itself. Clarity, timbre, reverberation, absorption, and reflection vary throughout the archiphonic scape, waiting to be explored by visitors and students alike, both within the interior and exterior of the building.

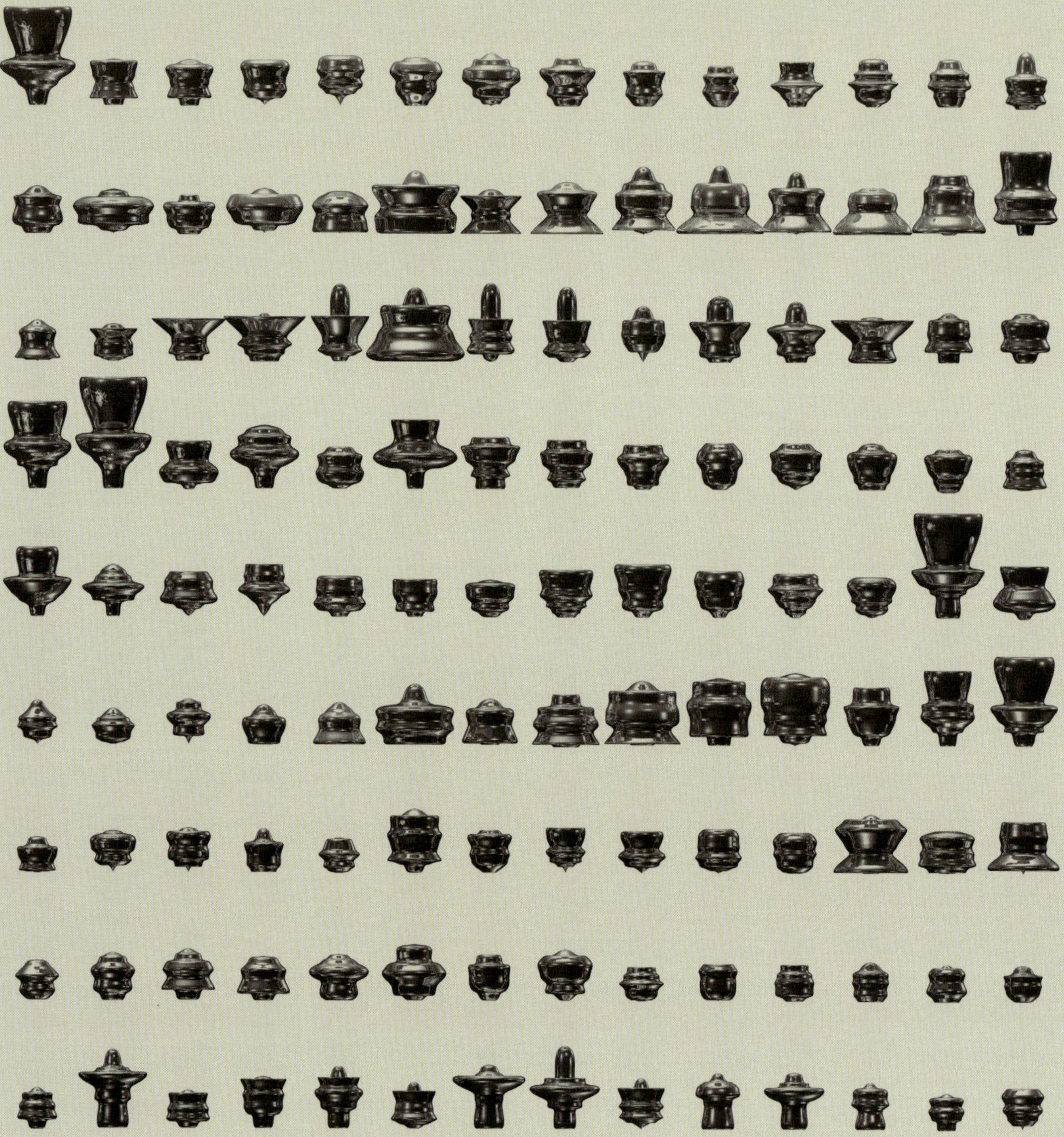

VESTIGE

242

Transactive_Landscapes

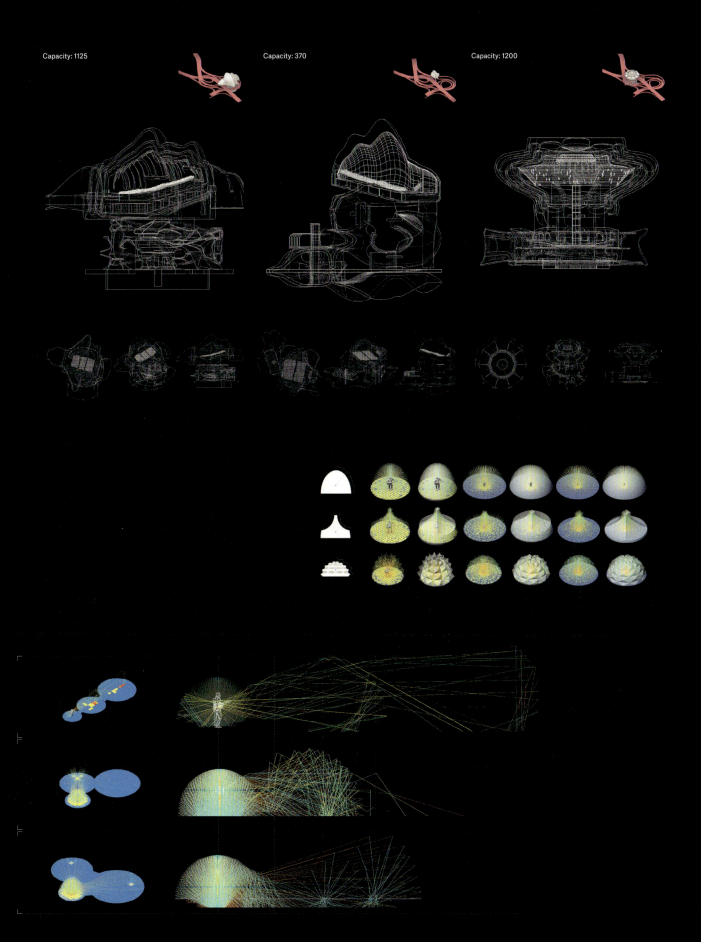

Re: Action

243

MIRABILIA
An Active Living System in the Post-Anthropocene

⊗ CHERNOBYL, UKRAINE

Angelica Lorenzi

244 Transactive_Landscapes

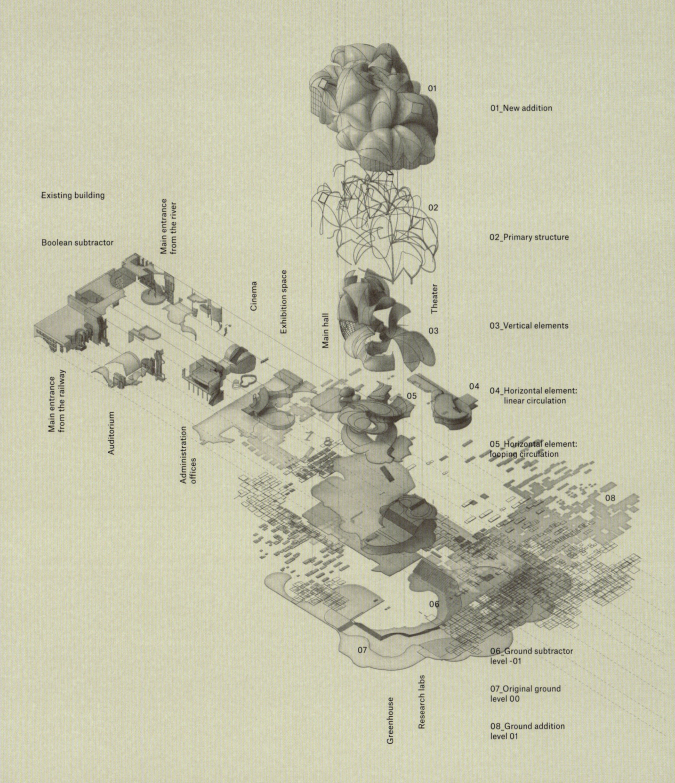

Re: Action

MIRABILIA

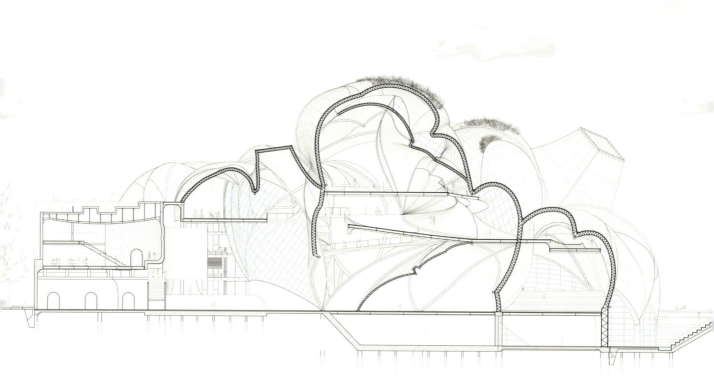

Transactive_Landscapes

INDULGENCE
A New Roman Bath House

⊗ VENICE, ITALY

Johanna Jelinek

INDULGENCE

[NO]WHERE
A New Habitat

⊗ SPITSBERGEN, NORWAY

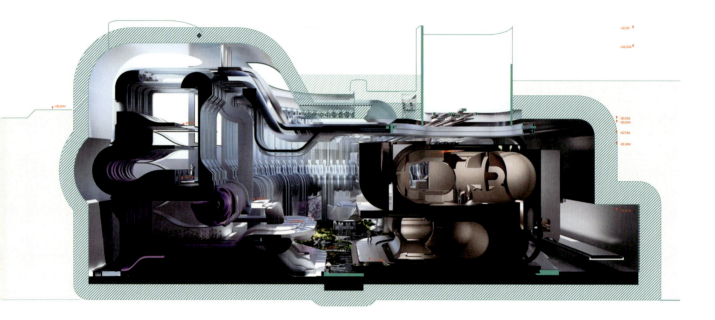

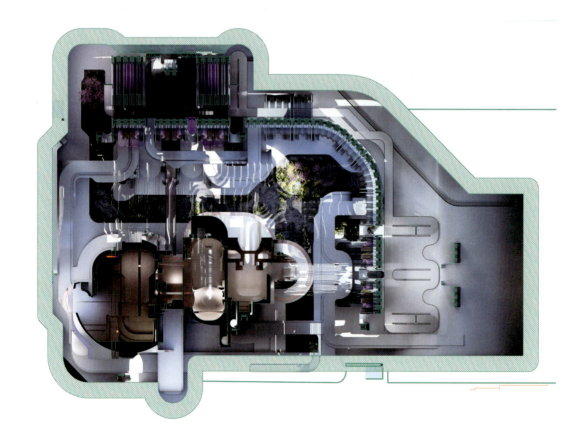

Leonie Eitzenberger, Kieran Tait

252 — Transactive_Landscapes

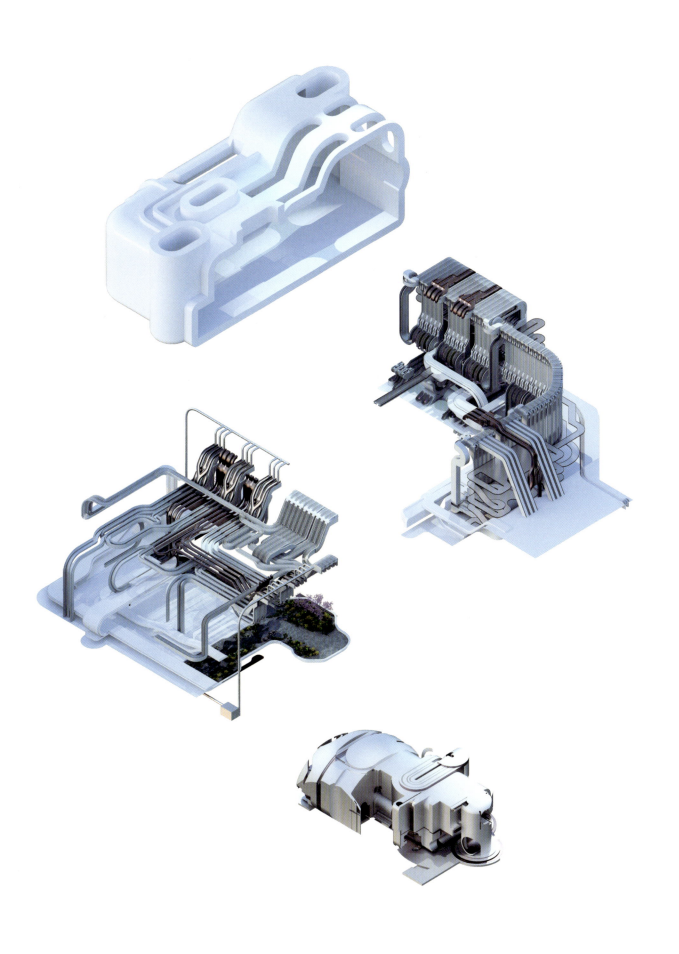

Re: Action

LOSTSCAPE
Experiential Observatory

⊗ NEVADA, USA

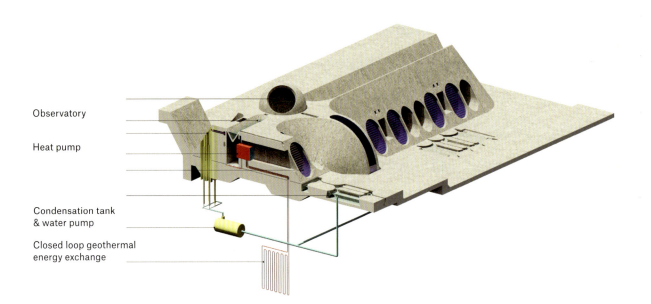

- Observatory
- Heat pump
- Condensation tank & water pump
- Closed loop geothermal energy exchange

Yana Ostapchuk

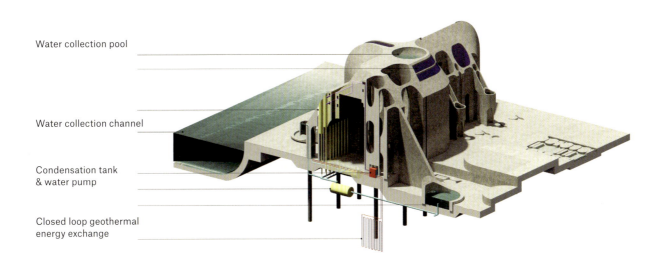

Water collection pool

Water collection channel

Condensation tank & water pump

Closed loop geothermal energy exchange

Re: Action

LOSTSCAPE

258   Transactive_Landscapes

MAKESHIFT GREAT AGAIN
An Expandable Hospital

⊗ GENEVA, SWITZERLAND

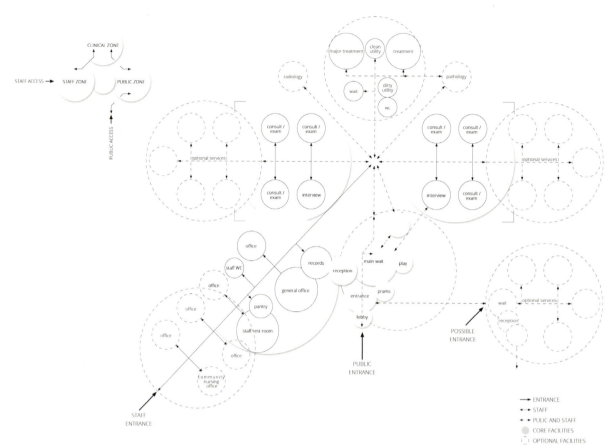

Functional Programming_Analysis

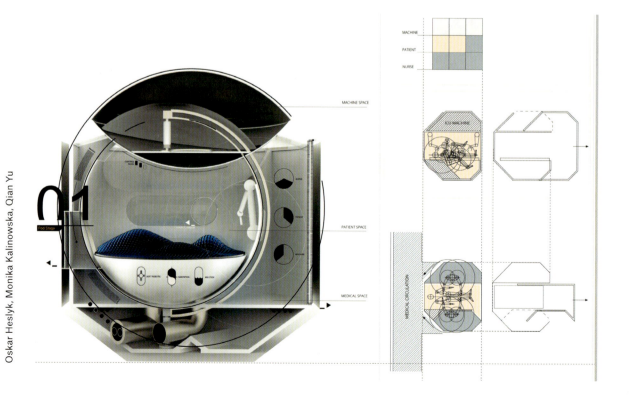

Stage2_Function Distribution

Oskar Heslyk, Monika Kalinowska, Qian Yu

Transactive_Landscapes

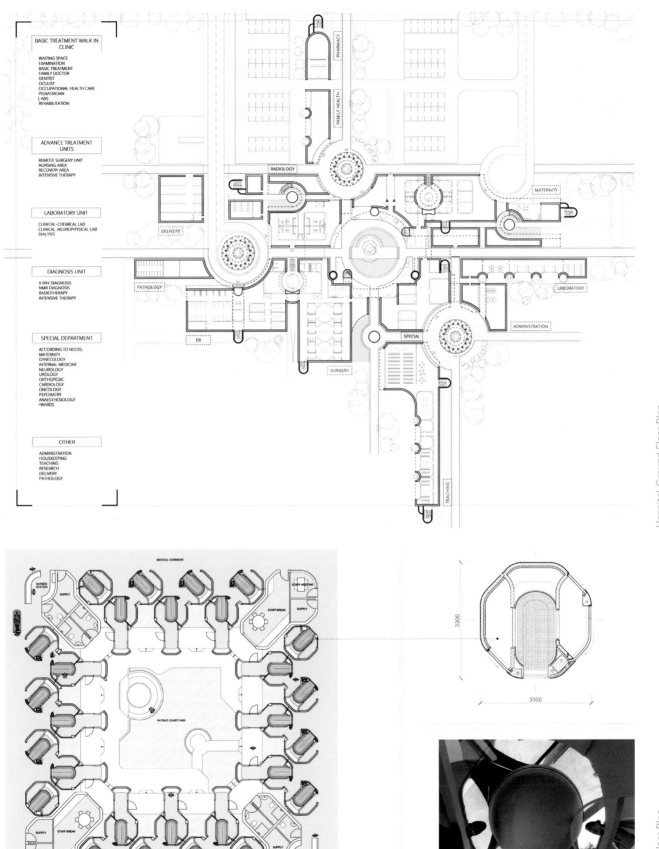

Hospital_Ground Floor Plan

Cluster_Floor Plan

Re: Action

08

Urban Agro_Culture

Agricultural production is one of humankind's most critical and primal necessities. Today's accelerated urbanization, predominantly driven by rapidly growing populations and mass migration to cities, must be tackled as this is one of the critical factors of increased greenhouse emissions and thereby a protagonist of global warming.

The exploitation and degradation of natural resources impacts natural ecosystems and perpetuates a vicious cycle of extreme climate fluctuations and random catastrophic ecological events. The resulting disruptions to agricultural and health-related systems often lead to water scarcity and food insecurity, giving rise to geopolitical conflicts and crises.

Today there is an imperative for health-oriented and nature-focused, domestic-scaled landscapes to form. Noise pollution, along with light pollution, is a fundamental issue that has traditionally been ignored. However, the migratory patterns of birds, the necessity for increased insect and bee populations, and so many other aspects concerning the natural environment, need to be part of a radical shift in thinking of how architects should interface with nature. Alongside these few examples there are others perhaps more subtle but equally critical in the necessity to repair and remedy how the built environment is planned, built, and utilized.

While today's ever-increasing cultivation of farmland is more-or-less bound to technological innovation, advanced urban centers seem to have lost a connection to food production and distribution. While agricultural needs define the industrial and post-industrial city, the added pressures of food scarcity, food deserts, and the like, have placed undue stresses on the role that architecture and urban planning can play, especially in addressing the allocations of land, urban settlements, agricultural infrastructure, and transportation networks. Sound models of urban expansion are more critical than ever as the necessity of negotiating ever-changing boundaries between rural and urban conditions becomes increasingly contentious. Today, architects have specific actions to undertake that are necessary to help achieve some semblance of food and water security. Visionary urban planning that can improve sustainable agricultural activity in a symbiotic relationship with urban centers is a crucial step.

Urban Agro_Culture interweaves projects that question the role of contemporary architecture in search of new modes of living and working while, at the same time, cultivating land and territories for food and other agricultural necessities. To accomplish this, looking at indigenous and local practices might garner a knowledge-based sustainable approach to design strategies. By strengthening community bonds, seeking ancient wisdom, or altering eating and living habits, the projects in this chapter rethink the future of food production and distribution as a symbiotic phenomenon with modernity and contemporary urban life. These projects carefully navigate the sometimes-blurred boundaries between urban and rural life in search of new typologies and methods for design approaches. They are based on approaches that tackle the intricacies of food and energy production, intertwining agricultural infrastructures such as greenhouses and growing fields to form a new kind of inspired city space. The key to these projects is the preoccupation with efficient and local strategies for resilient and sustainable agriculturally based urbanism.

THE MEAT MARKET
An Economical Catalyst
for the City of Detroit

⊗ DETROIT, USA

The project "The Meat Market—An Economical Catalyst for the City of Detroit" is located on the historical grounds of the Highland Park Ford Plant in Michigan, USA.

It was here where Henry Ford and his engineers developed many of the crucial principles of modern mass production, such as the first implementation of the assembly line.[1]

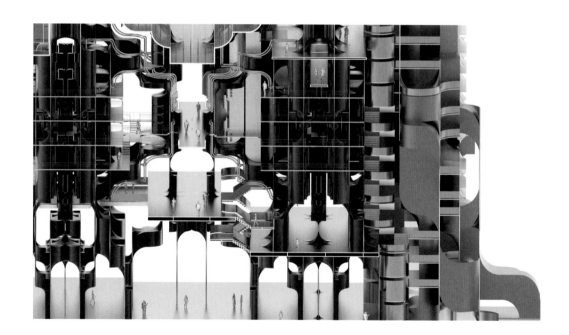

Barbara Schickermüller

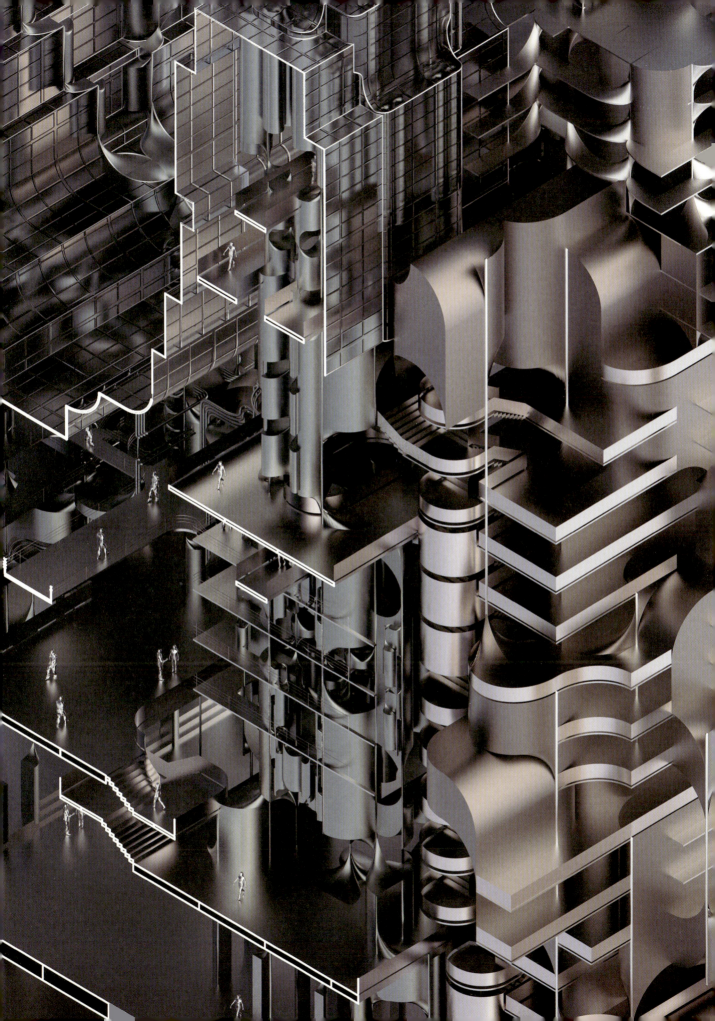

THE MEAT MARKET

Since those glory days in the beginning of the 20th century, a lot has changed in Detroit and its suburbs. The car industry collapsed due to decentralization, automatization of processes and the energy and economic crises. The population decreased from almost two million people to 700,000, with a lot of people living under the poverty line. 85% of all houses are abandoned; population density has decreased to less than 5,000 people per square mile.

With this low density also came the problem of food deserts. Almost half of all households are food insecure, which means that they live more than half a mile away from the next supermarket. Therefore, the city has also developed a huge lack of accessibility to healthy food, which has resulted in a rise in obesity and illness. Ironic, because before becoming a car-industry city, Detroit was the center of a diverse regional food economy.

In the past few years, in order to work against these problems, locals have started to grow their own vegetables and fruit in their backyards, benefitting from vacant plots everywhere within the city. Following this movement, more than 1,400 urban farms, community and school gardens have been built.

What is still missing is a sustainable source for growing meat, as currently most meat in supermarkets comes from all over the US and globe, adding a lot of food miles and, therefore, also greenhouse gas emissions. In addition to these well-known problems, the global livestock system has been causing, and contributing immensely to, climate change for a long time.

Humanity is growing, whereas available agricultural land is decreasing. Consumption habits are going to change; the demand for meat is generally increasing in the world. We are forced to look for new, more sustainable ways to feed humanity.

"Cultured meat" could be a solution: artificial meat that comes from stem cells that grow, develop, and expand within bioreactors, in combination with a liquid-nutrient serum. Compared to real meat like beef, pork, or chicken, it is way more efficient in terms of energy consumption, water use, land use, emissions etc. Studies suggest it is even healthier when compared to the traditional meat-production process. The artificial meat-growing lab skips the animal cruelty of barn-breeding, feed lots, and slaughtering.

The Meat Market is a prototype of the first artificial mass-meat production plant worldwide. The idea is to create a local food hub that combines two typologies: a traditional market and a state-of-the-art industrial food-production plant focusing on sustainable cultured meat. By bringing urban agriculture and environmentally friendly food production back into the city, where most of our food is consumed, the project not only reduces the ecological consequences of today's food consumption, but also intensifies the relationship between product and consumer again.

THE MEAT MARKET   Through its vertical approach, the assembly line makes use of gravity and new cutting-edge technologies—a vertical "growing" line for meat production that increases its efficiency while reducing its footprint. One vertical lab consists of different tank typologies such as a water tank, storage tank, cooling tank, and bioreactors in composition with structural elements and pipes that connect all of them. The tanks are arranged chronologically, starting with the first fluid "ingredients" on top, and then drip through to the next step, mimicking the principle of a sand clock. Eventually they arrive in the basement, where the finished product is then stored and/or immediately consumed or sold on the market.

As a factory building that needs to be able to meet and adapt to the current demands of the people, The Meat Market was conceptualized as a modular structure. Each module consists of four vertical meat-growing labs that are connected by a sustainable energy-supply system and supported by research labs, restaurants, an office space and market. In a future scenario, a network of meat production plants could potentially be developed throughout the city, intervening in the most critical areas such as low-income neighborhoods with a lack of access to healthy and sustainable food.

The Meat Market therefore also aims to make a major long-term contribution to the long recovery process of Detroit's economy.

1   "Highland Park Ford Plant," National Park Service U.S. Department of the Interior, October 16, 2007, www.nps.gov/nr/travel/detroit/d32.htm.

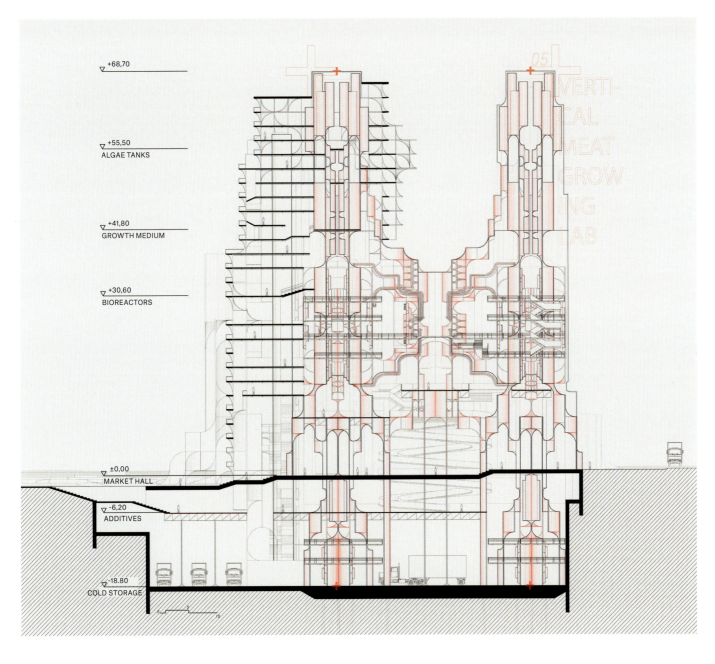

The idea is to create a local food hub that combines two typologies: a traditional market and a state-of-the-art industrial food-production plant focusing on sustainable cultured meat.

TEMPLE OF FOOD
Urban Food Production Hub

⊗ VIENNA, AUSTRIA

Alexander Ahmad

272 — Urban Agro_Culture

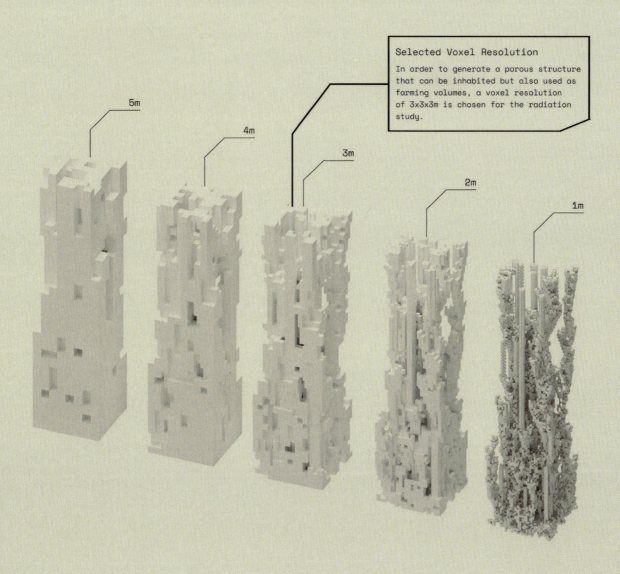

A local strategy that can be adapted to different geographical positions and weather scenarios. The generative growth process is being used to generate porous tower structures that can be filled with plants as an urban vertical farming solution.

Selected Voxel Resolution

In order to generate a porous structure that can be inhabited but also used as farming volumes, a voxel resolution of 3x3x3m is chosen for the radiation study.

TEMPLE OF FOOD

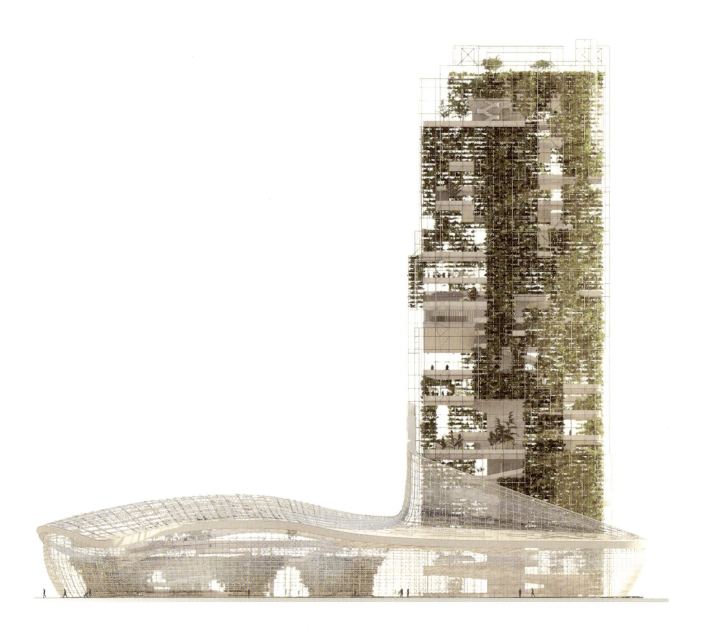

274　　　　　　　　　　Urban Agro_Culture

TRACES
Trouble in the Away Away

⊗ DHAKA, BANGLADESH

"Traces: Trouble in the Away Away" proposes a concept for a medicinal plant repository in Bangladesh that explores the future pharmaceutical possibilities of combining Ayurveda and Western medicine. The instigating premise of the project is based on the ecological crisis we currently find ourselves in and how architecture can become an approach to co-exist with it. To confront this topic, the project takes place in Bangladesh—often referred to as "ground zero for climate change"[1]—specifically Dhaka, because of the intersection between its high-risk climate zone status, abundance of naturally growing medicinal plants, and rapid urban expansion and dense population.

Jade Bailey

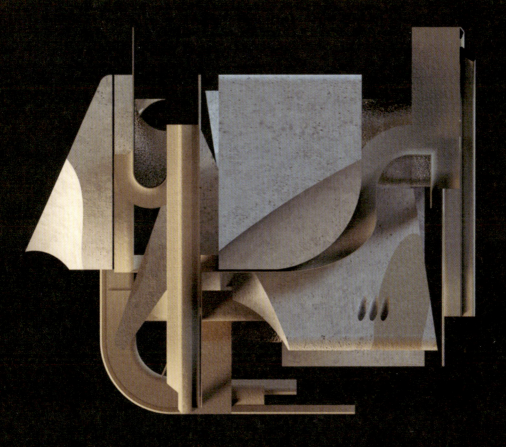
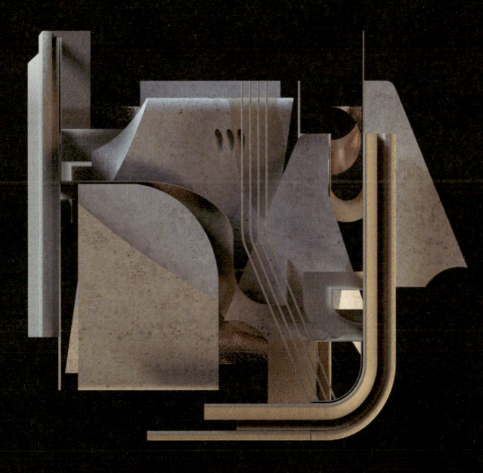

TRACES

Bangladesh is home to thousands of medicinal plants that are at risk due to the eradication of their natural ecosystems.[2] With predictions estimating a loss of one third of all plant species within the next fifty years alone[3] and the loss of one major drug species every two years,[4] it is important that action be taken to preserve them. "Traces: Trouble in the Away Away" proposes an architectural design to house this pursuit of pharmacognosy by creating spaces to cultivate and advance traditional methods of Ayurveda—native natural medicine—whilst combining it with the technology and knowledge of Western medicine to create a hybrid between the two. The intention is to create a hub of medicinal research to both discover and create habitats for medicinal plants so that they can be preserved, researched, and deployed to the local community and so that the cultural importance of alternative medicine can be maintained in the future of pharmaceutical structures.

To achieve this, the building includes gardens that house different biomes, laboratories, a small manufacturing center, academic facilities along with treatment pavilions for locals. The spatial programs interlink and connect by means of visibility and frequent circulation confluence points to allow cross-pollination between the users in order to share knowledge and ultimately open the currently closed demeanor of the pharmaceutical world. An association with trust and

The proposal outlines a concept for a medicinal plant repository in Bangladesh that seeks to explore the future pharma of combining Ayurveda and Western medicine.

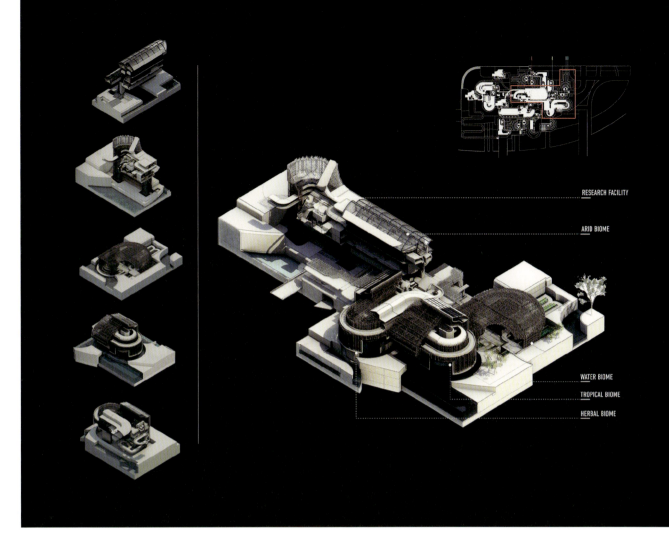

exposure was a core objective in the architectural intent, and so having interlinked spaces with visible sightlines and adjacencies is crucial to how the building is laid out and developed. The design is based on a compartmental design, with each biome and architectural component having its own research facility, public garden, and seed bank. The architectural components interlock where the labs are located, meaning that private passages for researchers, scientists and horticulturists can happen within the center of the building, more efficiently and within an enclosed and controlled environment, whilst the public route meanders through the biome gardens. The programmatic buildup from public to private therefore works its way inwards as it transitions from public gardens to research spaces.

The design incorporates architectural scenarios for four different biomes: Arid, Herbal, Tropical, and Water-based, of which each correlates to a current vegetative ecosystem found in Bangladesh. Because of the country's size and location, the environmental conditions in which the plants grow optimally vary quite substantially. These conditions are achieved within the proposal by specific positioning on site, elevation, and material, designed via analysis, to accentuate the natural climate by using varying degrees of shading and enclosure to induce the right degrees of solar radiation, humidity, and heat, minimizing the use of artificially conditioned and enclosed spaces which work together as one system. This eliminates the need to heat and cool the building mechanically. All biomes are elevated from the ground, separate from the water gardens, to preempt the inevitability of flooding in the future, and therefore maintain the integrity of the system as a whole.

Materials have become one of the new frontiers of architectural design. Now more than ever the relationship between the built form, human inhabitants, and its compositional substance is being questioned, explored, and developed, instigated by the climate crisis and advanced through computational design.

TRACES

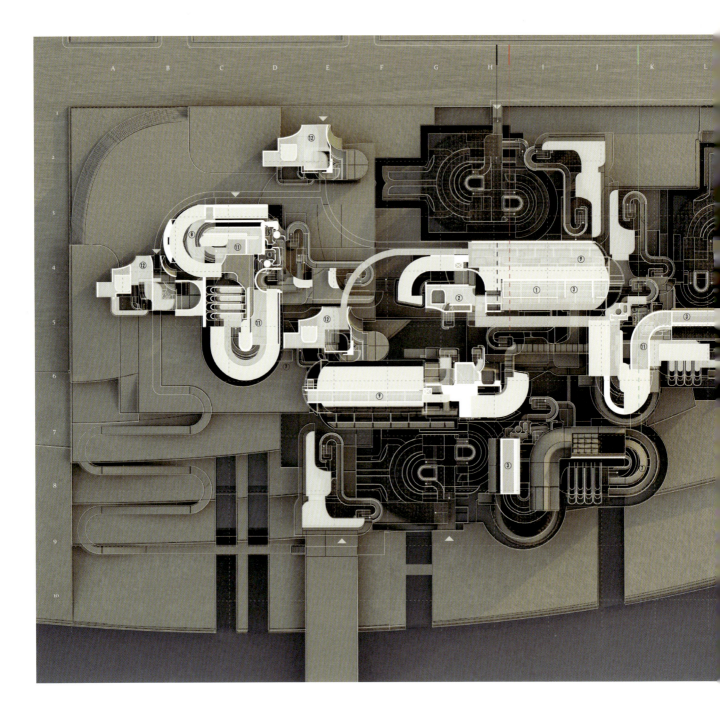

Urban Agro_Culture

The building materials are sourced and fabricated locally, giving the building an essence of belonging and eliminating the aspect of Awayness.[5] "Traces" highlights three bio-fabricated and local materials to address this, using natural elements from the surrounding environs that are residues from the encroaching global climate change and warming. Through materiality, the design offers a path of architectural reconciliation by "combining digital literacy with environmental consciousness"[6] to instill ecological awareness. The integration of bio-fabrication techniques, working with natural composite materials, and localizing the construction material and manufacturing process are aspects of the design integral to designing with a non-carbon future in mind.

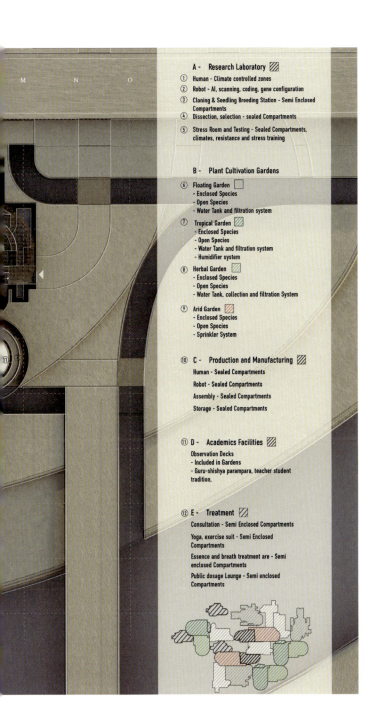

1   "Global Climate Index 2021," www.germanwatch.org/en/cri, accessed July 2, 2022.
2   "Annals of Agricultural Sciences," Science Direct, www.sciencedirect.com/science/article/pii/S0570178318300150, accessed July 2, 2022.
3   "Recent Responses to Climate Change Reveal the Drivers of Species Extinction and Survival," www.pnas.org/doi/10.1073/pnas.1913007117, accessed July 2, 2022.
4   "Nature's Pharmacy, Our Treasure Chest: Why We Must Conserve Our Natural Heritage," www.biologicaldiversity.org/publications/papers/Medicinal_Plants_042008_lores.pdf, accessed July 2, 2022.
5   Timothy Morton, "Architecture without Nature," Tarp: Architectural Manual: Not Nature (July 2017).
6   Antoine Picon, Beyond Digital Avant-Gardes: The Materiality of Architecture and Its Impact (Hoboken: John Wiley & Sons Ltd, 2020).

Re: Action

AGRO PRAXIS
Advanced Farming Systems

⊗ N'DJAMENA, CHAD

"Agro Praxis" envisions an adaptive agricultural system/platform to adapt to the consequences of climate change in N'Djamena, Chad. There is mounting evidence that climate change will unquestionably result in new realities in the immediate future, fundamentally changing the means of being. From predictions that inform the different realities humanity will face, we have to form robust scenarios where we could adapt to perform under these predetermined consequences and assist societies to become more resilient.

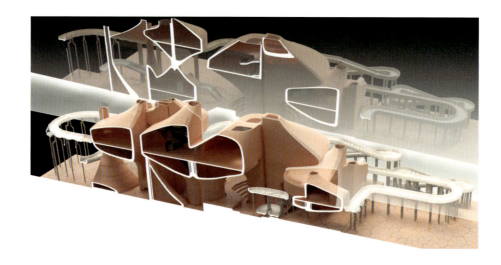

Nikita Ponomarev, Adham Sinan Hamedaat, Alexandra Terekhova

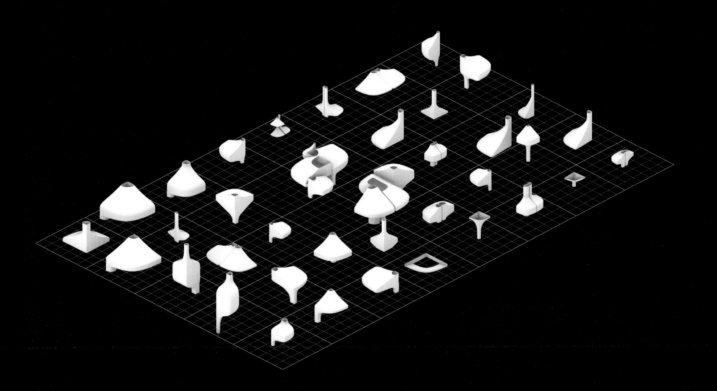

Agro Praxis

The site is located on the delta of the Chahri River—at the meeting point of the Chahri and Lagoon rivers in Chad's capital, N'Djamena—on the natural border with Cameroon. The site has historically been used for agricultural activities. Characteristically, as the location indicates, it is prone to flooding that further contributes to the fertility of the soil. The site is within close proximity to the capital city's center and hosts vital functions related to livestock and crops between Cameroon and Chad, the central trade hub for Chad at large.

Considering that Central Africa and the Sahel region's temperature rise caused by climate change is expected to be double the worldwide average, humidity will also increase as a result, making usual agricultural practices challenging. With the Sahel region experiencing increasing temperatures 1.5 times faster than the world average, air humidity and evapotranspiration, according to UNHCR reports, are consequently projected to increase, while soil moisture will decrease, contributing to lesser and lesser yields as the climate crisis unfolds.

Urban Agro_Culture

This intervention intends to provide people with advanced farming systems, bringing significantly increased yields. It also includes educational facilities to train farmers and support their families, as well as markets and research centers to create a sustainable environment.

The overall objective of the project is to look at challenges as untapped potentials. When adopting this strategy, one could envisage viable future scenarios where affected societies can adapt and become resilient in the light of the predetermined issues posed by the climate crisis. Climate change is a threat multiplier with many models pointing toward the direct relationship between climate change and conflict, and drivers ranging from rising temperatures to water insecurity and drought. This project defines climate change's adverse consequences and predictions as a potential to find new ways to coexist with climate change by coupling vernacular architecture and available technology, envisioning an architectural system in N'Djamena, Chad that is circular in nature, sufficient, and sensitive to the complex problems presented by overlapping contexts.

Locality is at the heart of the project, emulating an architecture that takes shape within the constraints of materiality, social structures, and environmental conditions, and therefore yields a style closely related to the vernacular. The project utilizes conventional building materials, i.e. clay, while providing a construction strategy that is commercially available such as clay 3D-printing and standardized architectural elements on one hand, while planning the logistics and circular nature of the master form on the other, such as excavation used for creating a terraced hybrid-farming system that also provides the building material.

Biographies
Studio Hani Rashid

HANI RASHID

Hani Rashid is a practicing architect and, together with Lise Anne Couture, co-founder of New York-based Asymptote Architecture. Asymptote has produced several significant projects worldwide, including the iconic Yas Marina Hotel built above the Abu Dhabi Formula One Race Circuit, the ARC, a contemporary Multimedia Arts Center in Daegu, South Korea, and most recently the ING Bank Headquarters in Gent, Belgium. Asymptote is currently building the new Sofitel Hotel in the center of Budapest at the historic Chain Bridge.

Alongside a distinguished professional career, Hani Rashid has held numerous professorships, including at the Royal Danish Academy, Princeton University and the ETH in Zurich, Switzerland. Hani was awarded the Kenzo Tange Chair for Architecture at Harvard's GSD and was an Associate Professor at Columbia's GSAPP, where he co-founded and developed the school's Advanced Digital Design Program. Hani Rashid is currently the head of Architectural Design Studio 3 Architectural Design Studio 3, a graduate design studio at the Institute of Architecture at the University of Applied Arts Vienna.

Hani Rashid's drawings, models, and works are included in several important museum collections, including the MoMA in New York, the Netherlands Institute of Architecture (NAI), the Pinakothek der Moderne in Munich, the San Francisco Museum of Modern Art, the Centre Pompidou in Paris, the Frac Centre in Orléans, France and the Solomon R. Guggenheim Museum in New York. The projects produced have been the subject of three monographs.

Hani Rashid has been a New York Foundation of the Arts Fellow, served on the steering committee for the international Aga Khan Award for Architecture, and was awarded the Luis Barragan Chair in Mexico. From 2013 until 2018, Hani was the Austrian Frederick and Lillian Kiesler Private Foundation President. In 2000 Hani Rashid, along with Greg Lynn, co-represented the United States at the 7th Venice Architecture Biennale, and in 2004 Hani Rashid and Lise Anne Couture were awarded the Frederick Kiesler Prize for Architecture and the Arts. Asymptote was named by TIME magazine as a Leader in Innovation for the 21st Century.

STUDIO TEAM SINCE 2016

SOPHIE C. GRELL

Sophie C. Grell is a licensed architect and member of the Austrian Federal Chamber of Architects and Engineers, where she is also a registered mediator in the planning, construction and environmental sectors. Sophie has been practicing in Vienna and teaching at the Institute of Architecture at the University of Applied Arts Vienna at Studio_Hani Rashid since 2011 and at the Institute of Urban Design (ioud), University of Innsbruck, Austria since 2019.

Sophie studied art history at the University of Vienna and architecture at UCLA, Los Angeles and the University of Applied Arts Vienna, where in 2006 she received her master's degree in architecture with distinction (Studio Wolf Prix). As a member of the Institute of Architecture, she was co-founder and chief editor of the Prinz Eisenbeton Magazine (2005–2011).

Sophie gained professional experience working as a design architect at COOP HIMMELB(L)AU in Vienna, Los Angeles and Mexico, where she was chief designer for numerous projects.

ELDINE HEEP

Eldine Heep is a Vienna-based architect. Since 2015, she has been teaching in the Studio of Hani Rashid at the Institute of Architecture at the University of Applied Arts Vienna. In her own spatial design practice, she is working on a wide range of projects at the inter-section of architecture, design, and art.

She studied architecture at the Academy of Fine Arts Vienna and the University of Applied Arts Vienna (Studio Zaha Hadid) where she received her master's degree (Mag. arch) with distinction. Subsequently she was awarded the MAK-Schindler residency scholar-ship in Los Angeles and her work has been exhibited in numerous group exhibitions. She gained professional experience working as a design architect at Labvert in Vienna and as a project architect and associate at Spark Architects in Beijing, China, where she worked on the design and execution of large-scale projects in Asia. Eldine is a licensed architect at the Austrian Federal Chamber of Architects and Engineers.

JOSE CARLOS LOPEZ CERVANTES

Jose Carlos Lopez Cervantes is a licensed architect and is currently working and teaching in Vienna and Innsbruck. He received his master's degree in architecture at the University of Granada, Spain. He holds a MSc from the University of Applied Arts Vienna. He is currently a PhD candidate with an international cotutelle between the University of Granada and the University of Innsbruck where he has a Senior Scientist teaching position. Previous teaching includes the Postgraduate Program of the University of Applied Arts Vienna, the Institute for Advance Architecture of Catalonia, the School of Architecture Technological University Lund, the University of Granada, and the Städelschule Architecture Class Frankfurt.

Jose worked at COOP HIMMELB(L)AU and he is cofounder of Studio Soqotra. His work has been exhibited at the Joanneum Museum Graz, the Austrian Pavilion at Venice Biennale 2010 and the Official Chamber of Architects. He has been a teaching member of Studio Hani Rashid since 2016.

SOPHIE LUGER

Sophie Luger is a licensed architect and member of the Austrian Federal Chamber of Architects and Engineers, currently working and teaching in Vienna. She studied at the UCL Bartlett School of Architecture in London and the University of Applied Arts Vienna, where she received her master's degree (Mag. arch) in architecture (Studio Zaha Hadid) in 2006. She obtained a grant from the Austrian Federal Ministry of Education, Arts, and Culture and gained professional experience as a design architect at Asymptote Architecture New York, Wolfgang Tschapeller ZT GmbH, and CAP Vienna, among others. Her work ranges from large-scale interventions to exhibition design and projects with a particular focus on sound behavior. She gained further academic qualification in acoustic building and sound performance in 2018.

LENIA MASCHA

Lenia Mascha is an architect currently teaching and practicing in Vienna. She is a member of the Institute of Architecture at the University of Applied Arts Vienna, teaching at Studio Hani Rashid since 2017 and conducting interdisciplinary research on architectural design and environmental acoustics. She is founder of the Vienna-based studio LNMSCH, focusing on design research in architecture and the arts. Previously, she taught design courses at the Institute of Urban Design at the University of Innsbruck (2016–2017) and co-directed the I oA traveling workshop at the Aristotle University of Thessaloniki (2018). She has been a senior design architect for over seven years at Berger+Parkkinen Architects and has collaborated with offices Asymptote Architecture NYC and CAP Architects. She studied architecture in Berlin, Vienna, and Thessaloniki and holds an architecture diploma and a postgraduate master's degree in urban strategies. She is a licensed architect and a member of the Technical Chamber of Greece. www.leniamascha.com

CLAUDIA RÜSSLI

Claudia Rüssli has studied at the Lucerne University of Applied Sciences and Arts – Engineering & Architecture (Switzerland) and holds a Bachelor of Arts in Architecture. Her studies focused on design and construction methodology, design and cultural understanding, implementation and construction, and interdisciplinary collaboration. She gained professional experience in various offices in Lucerne and Zurich, where she was involved in the planning and execution of a wide variety of projects as a project manager. Since 2020 she lives in Vienna and works as Studio Manager at Studio Hani Rashid.

ANDREA TENPENNY

From 2013 until 2022, she was the Administrator at Studio Hani Rashid, responsible for organizational matters, as well as public relations and events.

Re: Action

Biographies
Panel Participants

ANAB JAIN

Anab Jain is a filmmaker, designer, and futurist.
She is the co-founder of Superflux, a pioneering speculative design and experiential futures company
in London, UK, working for clients and commissioners
such as V&A, Google, Red Cross, UNDP, IKEA,
Deepmind and many more. Anab has delivered prolific
talks at TED, Skoll, NEXT, The House of Lords and
The House of Commons in the UK, and has shown work
at MoMA New York, V&A London, National Museum
of China and Museum of the Future in Dubai. Profiles
on Anab and Superflux can be found in the Wall Street
Journal, Business Insider and Financial Times.

Anab is also a Professor for Design Investigations
at the University of Applied Arts Vienna.
Her work can be found at www.superflux.in.
You can follow her on Twitter: @anabjain

GREG LYNN

Greg Lynn is the founder and owner of Greg Lynn FORM.
He has served on numerous advisory boards and
is co-founder and CEO of the robotic company Piaggio
Fast Forward. He is o. Univ. Prof. Arch. and head of Studio
Lynn at the I oA, University of Applied Arts Vienna
and a Professor at UCLA. He won a Golden Lion at the
Venice Biennale of Architecture and has represented
the United States in the American Pavilion at the Venice
Biennale of Architecture twice. His architectural work
is in the permanent collections of museums including
the CCA, SFMoMA, ICA Chicago and MoMA New York;
and his Alessi "Supple" Mocha Cups and Vitra "Ravioli"
Chair have been inducted into the Museum of Modern
Art's Permanent Collection. He received the American
Academy of Arts & Letters Architecture Award, is the
recipient of a Red Dot Best of the Best Design Award
and was awarded a fellowship from United States Artists.
He is the author of thirteen books. He was born in 1964.
In 1986, he graduated from Miami University of Ohio
with Bachelor of Environmental Design and Bachelor
of Philosophy degrees, and in 1988 he graduated from
Princeton University with a Master of Architecture degree.

TIMOTHY MORTON

Timothy Morton is Rita Shea Guffey Chair in English at Rice University. They have collaborated with Laurie Anderson, Björk, Jennifer Walshe, Hrafnhildur Arnadottir, Sabrina Scott, Adam McKay, Jeff Bridges, Olafur Eliasson, Pharrell Williams, and Justin Guariglia. Morton co-wrote and appears in *Living in the Future's Past*, a 2018 film about global warming with Jeff Bridges. They are the author of the libretto for the opera *Time Time Time* by Jennifer Walshe.

Morton has written *All Art Is Ecological* (Penguin, 2021), *Spacecraft* (Bloomsbury, 2021), *Hyposubjects: On Becoming Human* (Open Humanities, 2021), *Being Ecological* (Penguin, 2018), *Humankind: Solidarity with Nonhuman People* (Verso, 2017), *Dark Ecology: For a Logic of Future Coexistence* (Columbia, 2016), *Nothing: Three Inquiries in Buddhism* (Chicago, 2015), *Hyperobjects: Philosophy and Ecology after the End of the World* (Minnesota, 2013), *Realist Magic: Objects, Ontology, Causality* (Open Humanities, 2013), *The Ecological Thought* (Harvard, 2010), *Ecology without Nature* (Harvard, 2007), eight other books, and 270 essays on philosophy, ecology, literature, music, art, architecture, design, and food. Morton's work has been translated into thirteen languages. In 2014 they gave the Wellek Lectures in Theory.

CLAUDIA PASQUERO

Claudia Pasquero is an architect, curator, author, and educator; her work and research operates at the intersection of biology, computation and design. She is co-founder of ecoLogicStudio in London, Landscape Architecture Professor at Innsbruck University and Associated Professor at the Bartlett UCL. Claudia was Head Curator of the Tallinn Architectural Biennale 2017, which she titled Bio-Tallinn, and was nominated in the WIRED smart list in the same year.

She is co-author of *Systemic Architecture: Operating Manual for the Self-Organizing City* published by Routledge in 2012, and is currently co-authoring her latest book *DeepGreen: Biodesign in the Age of Artificial Intelligence*, due to be published in autumn 2023. Her work has been exhibited internationally: at the Centre Pompidou in Paris, the Design Museum in London, the Venice Architecture Biennale, the Mori Museum in Tokyo, ZKM Karlsruhe, the Saudi Design Festival in Riyadh, COP26 in Glasgow, and Hyundai Motorstudio in Korea among others. ecoLogicStudio has successfully completed a series of Photo.Synthetica architectures, such as the Urban Algae Folly Milano 2015, the BioTechHut Astana 2017, PhotoSynthEtica Dublin 2019 and Helsinki 2020, AirBubble Playground Warsaw 2021, AirBubble inflatable eco-machine in Glasgow/Riyadh 2022 and Cairo 2023, the Air Lab in London, and Tree One in Busan 2023.

Students
2011–2023

Mohamed ABDELHADY OMAR
Sarah AGILL
Alex AHMAD
Haitham AL BUSAFI
Lea ARTNER
Jade BAILEY
Ioana BINICA
Adriana BÖCK
Kyle BRANCHESI
Louis BRAUNGER
Peregrine BUCKLER
Hümeyra CAM
Jarrod CARANTO
Arpapan CHANTANAKAJORNFUNG
Kaveh CHEHRI
Meltem ÇINAR
Dor COHEN
Joseph COOK
Cristina CORTUTA
Johannes CZIEGLER
Goni DAGAN
Ivo DE NOOIJER
Lea DIETIKER
Kyryll DMYTRENKO
Ibrokhimbek DUSMUKHAMEDOV
Vojislav DZUKIC
Olavur EGHOLM
Leonie EITZENBERGER
Alejandro ESTRELLA
Tilman FABINI
Hessamedin FANA
Florian FEND
Abraham FUNG
Lisa Marie GERDES
Benjamin GÖRN
Hulda GUDJONSDOTTIR
Fady HADDAD
Alexander HAID
Roman HAJTMANEK
Adham Sinan HAMEDAAT
Oliver HAMEDINGER
Moritz HANSHANS
Oskar HESLYK
Harry HINTON-HARD

Kojiro HONDA
Josh HOROVITZ
Mary HUGHES
Ludmila JANIGOVA
Johanna JELINEK
Witchaya JINGJIT
Olivia JOIKITS
Gakku JUMANIYASOVA
Mathias JUUL FROST
Monika KALINOWSKA
Dennis KARANDIUK
Nikola KÁRNÍKOVÁ
Elizaveta KARPACHEVA
Leonard KERN
Joonghoon KIM
David KIPP
Jinhee KOH
Polina KOROCHKOVA
Melanie KOTZ
Jan KOVÁŘÍČEK
Magdalena KRASKA
Paul KRIST
Lena KRIWANEK
Jon KRIZAN
Anders KROGH
Arian LEHNER
Ewa LENART
Angelica LORENZI
Miriam LÖSCHER
Dan LU
Yi-Chen LU
Guillaume MACÉ
Saba MAHDAVI
Jalal MATRAJI
Steven MATTI
Peter MEARS
Luca MELCHIORI
Alec MELKONIAN
Anais MÉON
Ondřej MICHÁLEK
Soroush NADERI
Kaveh NAJAFIAN
Alexander NANU
Silvia NANU

Yana OSTAPCHUK
Sadi ÖZDEMIR
Shpend PASHTRIKU
Sonali PATEL
Christoph PEHNELT
Lenka PETRÁKOVÁ
Sille PIHLAK
Noemi POLO
Anutorn POLPHONG
Nikita PONOMAREV
Andjela POPOVIC
Mihai POTRA
Luis Daniel POZO
Piotr Konstanty PROKOPOWICZ
Daniel PROST
Olja RADOVANOVIC
Jean-Philipp REINSBERG
Daniel RHOMBERG
Maximin RIEDER
Stephan RITZER
Jeroen Hendrik S. ROOSEN
Kristína RYPÁKOVÁ
Andrea SACHSE
Dena SAFFARIAN
Viktória SÁNDOR
Emma SANSON
Sharon SARFATI
Jaanika SAU
Herwig SCHERABON
Dennis SCHIAROLI
Barbara SCHICKERMÜLLER
Simon SCHÖMANN
Lewis SCOTT
Adam SEBESTYEN
Anastasia SHESTERIKOVA
Gisle SIMONSEN
Klemens SITZMANN
Anastasia SMIRNOVA
Artur STAŠKEVITŠ
Ralph S. STEENBLIK
Raffael STEGFELLNER
Andrej STRIEŽENEC
Colby SUTER
Simonas SUTKUS

Kieran TAIT
Johan TALI
Matthew TAM
Alexandra TEREKHOVA
Stefan THANEI
Stefanie THEURETZBACHER
Patricia TIBU
Ursula TROST
Anna TUZOVA
Nora VARGA
Robert VIERLINGER
Jiri VITEK
Jelena VUKMIROVIC
Anna WAWRZYNIAK
Simon WEISHÄUPL
Markus WILLEKE
Ryan WYNN
Shilun YANG
Angel YONCHEV
Qian YU
Helena YUN
Arkady ZAVIALOV
Minerva ZHANG
Zhiyi ZHANG
Gaowei ZHOU

Imprint

EDITOR
Hani Rashid

EDITING TEAM
Sophie C. Grell, Eldine Heep,
Jose Carlos Lopez Cervantes,
Sophie Luger, Lenia Mascha

EDITORIAL ASSISTANCE
Claudia Rüssli

Studio Hani Rashid
I oA, Institute of Architecture,
University of Applied Arts Vienna,
Oskar-Kokoschka-Platz 2, A-1010 Vienna
studio-hani-rashid.at
studio.rashid@uni-ak.ac.at

PROJECT MANAGEMENT
"Edition Angewandte" on behalf of
the University of Applied Arts Vienna
Roswitha Janowski-Fritsch, A-Vienna

CONTENT AND PRODUCTION EDITOR
ON BEHALF OF THE PUBLISHER
Katharina Holas, A-Vienna

PROOFREADING/COPYEDITING
Alun Brown, Scott Clifford Evans

GRAPHIC DESIGN
Bleed (Marc Damm, Astrid Feldner)

PRINTING
Holzhausen, die Buchmarke der Gerin Druck GmbH, A-Wolkersdorf

PAPER
Claro Bulk 135 g/m², Surbalin Honan Diamant 115 g/m²

TYPEFACE
Atlas Grotesk

The editors of this book have taken the utmost care
of ascertaining the identity of all holders of rights
to use the pictorial material in this book. All images
that do not contain a reference to the author are
Copyright Studio Hani Rashid.

LIBRARY OF CONGRESS CONTROL NUMBER
2022948102

Bibliographic information published by the German National Library
The German National Library lists this publication in the Deutsche
Nationalbibliografie; detailed bibliographic data are available on the
Internet at http://dnb.dnb.de.

This work is subject to copyright. All rights are reserved, whether
the whole or part of the material is concerned, specifically
the rights of translation, reprinting, re-use of illustrations, recitation,
broadcasting, reproduction on microfilms or in other ways,
and storage in data bases. For any kind of use, permission
of the copyright owner must be obtained.

ISSN 1866-248X
ISBN 978-3-0356-2707-7
e-ISBN (PDF) 978-3-0356-2710-7

© 2023 Birkhäuser Verlag GmbH, Basel
P.O. Box 44, 4009 Basel, Switzerland
Part of Walter de Gruyter GmbH, Berlin/Boston

987654321 www.birkhauser.com